CREATIVE INTENTION:
About Audiovisual Communication

From Hollywood to John Doe

by

BEN PARKER

and

PATRICIA DRABIK

Ph.D., University of Illinois

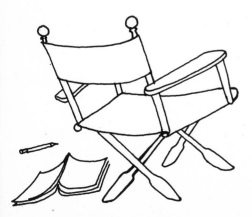

Library of Congress Cataloging in Publication Data

Parker, Ben.
　　Creative intention: from Hollywood . . . to John Doe.
　　1. Moving-pictures—Production and direction.
　　2. Television—Production and direction.
I. Drabik, Patricia, joint author.　II. Title.
PN1995.9.P7P3　　　791.43 '023　　　73-13509
ISBN 0-88238-054-0

Printed in the United States of America

Art Director
Je' Faulkner

Illustrators
William Brown,
Je' Faulkner

Edited by
JOSEPH TAUBMAN

Editorial Assistant
GAIL J. TOUSEY

To
a good friend and colleague
ARTHUR RIPLEY
"Teacher of scholars, servant of students"

TABLE OF CONTENTS

PART ONE: FROM HOLLYWOOD

1

PART TWO: TO JOHN DOE

—ACKNOWLEDGMENT—

The authors would like to express their appreciation and gratitude to the following "Creative Originators and Interpreters," who have given invaluable counsel in interviews, discussions and correspondence.

(The symbol * denotes Academy Award Winner.)

*GEORGE CUKOR, director—STANLEY CORTEZ, ASC, director of photography, contributor to Encyclopedia Britannica—*EDWARD DYMTRYK, producer, director and screen writer—*JOHN DUNNING, film editor —*JOHN HUSTON, producer director and screen writer—*HENRY KING, producer and director—*MERVYN LEROY, producer, director and screen writer—*JOSHUA LOGAN, producer, director and screen writer—KENNETH MACGOWAN, theatrical educator, author, screen writer and producer—DANIEL MANN, director—*LEO MCCAREY, director—*VINCENTE MINELLI, director—TED POST, live and film television director—ARTHUR RIPLEY, film editor, educator and screen writer—*MARK ROBSON, producer director and screen writer — *JOSEPH RUTTENBERG, ASC, director of photography—*GEORGE STEVENS, producer, writer and director—*DANIEL TARADASH, screen writer, (1969-1973) president, Screen Writers Guild of America)—*BILLY WILDER, producer, director and screen writer—*ROBERT WISE, producer, writer and director—*WILLIAM WYLER, writer and director—*FRED ZINNEMANN, producer and director.

The authors would also like to express their appreciation to the following producing organizations for their cooperation:

WARNER BROTHERS — COLUMBIA PICTURES — METRO-GOLDWYN-MAYER — TWENTIETH CENTURY FOX — PARAMOUNT — and UNIVERSAL INTERNATIONAL.

A special note of appreciation to Arthur Ripley, colleague at U.C.L.A., for permission granted to include excerpt of his scenario, "THE CHOSEN" in CREATIVE INTENTION.

❋   ❋   ❋

PREFACE

The materials embodied in this book have been used successfully as an aid to production for motion picture and other audio-visual media and in teaching by the authors in film, television, theatre and communications.

CREATIVE INTENTION is prepared not merely to explain or define, but to provoke thought, stimulate imagination, encourage "self" interpretation and expression.

Who is John Doe? Why is this book addressed to him? What have Hollywood and John Doe in common? What CREATIVE INTENTION can Hollywood translate for John Doe? How does John Doe discover the CREATIVE INTENTION of the originator and interpreter?

This book answers these questions from a professional point of view. It tells how CREATIVE INTENTION can be recognized and developed in every step of a production, from it's writing to its discovery by the audience.

Part I

Chapter 1

INTRODUCTION

The Significance of Creative Intention

INTRODUCTION

Man complicates life, and so it becomes complex. Many tales and story inventions are discovered in the "complications" of man and the resulting complexity.

Through the ages, man has endeavored to communicate whether by unintelligible grunts, gestures, drawings or by re-enactment. As life became more complicated, he tried to find out more about himself. Man is interested in man. He wants to know what makes him tick. What motivates and drives him as an individual? What shapes his relationship to his environment—the nature of his physical being, society and its many groups?

The world of the individual human being is unique even though there are billions of humans on earth. Some live more in the conflicts they bring about themselves, while others live to save them from their struggles and confusion. Some are motivated to create so that others may enjoy life, comfort and security. Some follow, like robots, without seeing, hearing, feeling or understanding much of what goes on around them. Some even destroy. And to some, life is meaningful only as a kaleidoscope of experiences.

Many people are questioning themselves and the world. The search for answers to these questions illuminates the conflicts from which theatre, in the largest sense, is created. It is with this aspect of theatre that this book is concerned, the theatre of the audio-visual media—film, television, tape, or any other processes or devices that technology may invent.

Volumes have been written about the techniques employed in audio-visual production. However, few authors have attempted to explore the fundamental problems faced by what we shall call the creative originator or interpreter.

Some of the content of this book represents the distillation of the experience of many distinguished professionals centered in Hollywood and the movie industry. It is now presented for the use of "John Doe," wishing to create for the audio-visual media.

We have not attempted to set down inexorable rules that must be followed. Instead we have defined elements which, with creative intention, the creative individual should consider in the origination of a production for any type of audio-visual medium.

Such definition is basic, for an individual's creativity must have a strong foundation from which it can grow. A creative originator may originate or create a story. He may also produce the story. It is possible that he may participate in a technical capacity, thereby creating a specific aspect of the production. He may even write the music. It is more likely to find each creative phase carried out by a different individual.

It is to the creator, whatever his contribution may be to the initiation and execution of a production, that this book is directed.

Each statement in this book has a reason and purpose. Challenge these statements if you wish. Test them by your own experience and practice. It is through the process of challenge and resolution that one comes to know the possibilities of one's own creative intention.

For creative intention is the purposeful planning of the elements of story and techniques of production to convey the creative individual's own interpretation to an audience.

Creativity, as it is related herein, is the process of thought and imagination which enables one to carry one's creative intention to an audience. The focus of creative intention is always the audience. We know that there are dimensions of experience within any given audience which the originator of a production cannot know or control. However, there are common elements of experience which can be used as a yardstick for selection of elements of story and production techniques, that will call forth the desired response in any given audience.

Without an audience, there is no creative intention. This book, therefore, is devoted to defining the ways by which an audience of the audio-visual media discovers the creative intent of the originator and interpreter through what it sees, hears and feels.

Chapter 2

INTERPRETATION . . . From Hollywood

APPROACH TO DIRECTING FOR
ALL MEDIA

APPROACH TO DIRECTION FOR ALL MEDIA

Interpretation

AN APPROACH TO DIRECTING

A DIRECTOR directs . . . an ACTOR acts—
They are interpretative artists

An audience, no matter which media it views, searches for interpretation of the story.

At present there are three main vehicles for story presentation: Motion Pictures, Television/Radio, and Theatre. One common denominator exists between the three: The art of what we refer to as "Theaterism". "Theaterism" is composed primarily of:

1. STORY

2. ACTORS

3. DIRECTOR

4. ARTISTIC ILLUSION

5. AUDIENCE

"Theaterism" is an expression of people by people for people. It is a way of life and because of its unique and complex structure, "theaterism" or "theatrical expression" requires a guide—a guide who not only can express the correct road to audience and actors alike, but molds and develops his charges along the way through knowledge, insight and sensitivity. This guide is the DIRECTOR and he is so called because he must understand interpretation of story and clearly convey it through the use of actors.

The art of interpretation lies in defining imagination. Artistic interpretation is a representation of the forceful imagination of an individual. It is expressed through individual style by one's own ingenuity and is defined by individual control. It originates in primitive reactions and is found in thoughts and ideas, sounds and meanings of words, and actions.

THE MEDIA—Domain of Artistic Expression

Although there are basic differences in the media of theatre, motion pictures and live television, acting techniques are similar and are framed by some kind of proscenium.

Making a film is artistic communication through composition. The artist must know analyze and visualize the story through his own imagination—point of view—in order to compose a picture which effects an intended response.

The film performs its function if it presents ideas and experiences with validity and credibility, and the requisite excitement to hold the viewer's attention.

People go to the cinema to see a world that isn't theirs—a world of experience, reality, or fantasy. More importantly they enter into a world of ideas not their own. The are exposed to ideas, thoughts and experiences without the wear and tear of living through them.

The making of a film story is the emergence of situations as a part of life. The composition must be directed to the problems of the story.

The FILM media offers a dual opportunity to produce works of art which make people think, and having thought, search their own minds, and to entertain for recreation, a laugh or even a good cry.

Film making is creative. The viewing of a film should be a subjective experience. Whether a film is designed to excite, amuse, or enlighten, it will not achieve its purpose unless the presentation can bring about emotional participation or audience identification with the characters, the theme, the plot and the situations in the story.

THEATRE can be said to be a "wide-frame" medium because the proscenium behind which the players perform does not, as does the camera, select the point of reference and emphasis for the viewer.

Selection on the stage is achieved through stagecraft and through the perspective of the actors' positions. While one actor is speaking, the others on stage are always in full view. This condition does not exist in film or in television, for these are intimately and exclusively selective media.

Film, in a sense, is a "close-up" medium since the camera can select close-ups and individual angles in greater or less detail, thereby directing and controlling audience emotions and attention.

LIVE TELEVISION has the same capability yet does not have the complete flexibility of the motion picture camera. In live television, it is virtually impossible to achieve a complete reverse-angle (the back wall) of a scene.

In the three media, the creation of a character by a performer requires a synthesis of intellectual and emotional responses to the story. However, in theatre production, such synthesis is evoked by the director and actor into a solid characterization. Thus the actor, in performance, is able to endow the character he is portraying with believability and sincerity.

In film, the actor performs without benefit of continuity playing. He creates his character in a step-by-step process and is dependent on the director to motivate him.

In live television, the approach to character development is similar to that of the theatre.

In film, theatre or live television, the director must project the theme and create the mood in order to dramatize. He must see the story as a drama, determine the order of motivation, then compose so as to dramatize. Motivation provides the continuity through which the story develops.

A director's job is to make the audience not only spectators, but to make them become a part of the story. The product of a director is for audience consumption, regardless of the medium employed.

WHAT IS DIRECTING?

DRAMATIZATION — MOTIVATION — COMPOSITION

Directing is both an art and a craft. Craftsmanship can be taught; artistic sensitivity is developed.

Before the director can practice his art or craft, he must understand the medium in which he works. He must have assimilated the principles that control the methods of his artistic expression. He must know how drama is created step by step, from the conception to the completion of a story.

The director in the film medium is a very special kind of artist—a very special student of the drama. His job is one of the hardest to keep, for often he is considered as good as his last assignment.

Directing, as such, has a long history of expressed theories and methods, but before the director can interpret the drama there are basic principles and concepts which he should know.

The director must be sensitive and receptive to the meaning of life. He must be able to respond easily and deeply to the joyful and the sorrowful, the good and the evil, the beautiful and the ugly. He must understand motivation, the meaning and the reason for action and the reaction. He must have individual conviction. He is the only person who can visualize the "whole" of the drama before it begins, as it develops and as it will finish.

A director should understand people, their drives, desires and responses. A director never stops learning. He should be aware of how experience shapes people and culture. He should not only know environment, but also how people live in their environment.

Directing is more than revealing a picture of things, or recording a truthful observation or the ordering of people to act and react. Directing is the art of impressing emotional meaning into an expression of life at the right moment.

Directing is an expression of interpretation which gives any form of art "life". The director should clearly interpret a story and motivate the actor to project an interpretation to the audience.

The director's job requires a number of strangely assorted and widely divergent abilities. He must be artist, critic, student and teacher.

INTENTION—Interpretation

The director should have the full use of his imagination in order to properly express his creative intention. The use of his imagination is a vivid process of "vitality", "touch", "feel", "spirit" and critical evaluation. The director can create a work of art by building story situations into dramatic, esthetic, and intellectual enjoyment for an audience.

The director must be a keen observer. Every experience, carefully observed and remembered, may be stored for future reference or use. The director is a student of human relations and audience psychology.

THE FILM DIRECTOR—Focuses upon his Audience

Directing in the film medium means interpreting to the actors and technicians how you, as a director, see the story and wish it told to the audience. In each and every situation, the director controls the continuous mood of every character. He plans the physical pacing of the scene.

It is the director, as the chief interpreter, who decides what the camera will do, what the microphone will take in and how the story will finally appear on the screen. The director should not simply point a camera at life and hope it will come out as a film.

To direct for the film medium one has to be able to utilize the creative functions of the technicians of sound, light, and design. He must have an understanding of editing problems and the principles of film editing. He must be conversant with elementary optics and the techniques of cinematography. Most important of all, he must have the ability to analyze and interpret story and character for an audience.

The director is also obliged to be a good administrator. He must be able to handle complex and sensitive characteristics in people. He must have clear-cut convictions, with an ability to recognize talent in others as well as to determine his own creative ability. He should be able to conduct himself with authority, responsibility and tact.

It is the duty of every director to carefully analyze the object of attention, the destination of the story and the intentions of the characters—in order to impress a theme, or an idea into a moving, colorful, dynamic presentation. This is accomplished through creative intention, which demands recognition and interpretation by the individual for an audience.

A DIRECTOR BEGINS

A director's job begins when the story begins, but his job does not end when the shooting is finished. He must constantly tell the story while he is preparing, shooting, editing, and showing it to an audience.

The director must learn, after he prepares the exposition, when to begin the story, for each story has a definite point at which it begins. He must also recognize when to end it. If it is ended improperly, his audience will react unfavorably and the theme will completely dissipate.

On the stage, during the rehearsals and before the cameras, the director must control the emotional pace of a scene. When an actor overacts, or underplays a scene, it is the director who must recognize such discrepancies and bring the actor's pace and emotion back where it belongs.

Acting is reacting to stimuli which help create the emotional beat. Emotional beat is a moment of discovery for the character portrayed by an actor.

The director is constantly his own "watch-dog", as he dictates and controls the emotional key of every single scene as it relates to the total story. In this way, he controls the photographic composition.

The director studies and determines the lighting so that it reveals the mood and helps tell the story. This can be accomplished by checking the scene through the camera's eye (the lens). He scrutinizes the proscenium which circumscribes the action, critically and thoughtfully to determine whether he is getting the desired composition.

Dramatization is a vital aspect of composition. From the outset, dramatization and characterization have to build, point-by-point. This is achieved by developing the various situations and arranging the story structure in a smooth and continuous flow of action.

A screen story demands motion. Motion expresses action through illusion and effect. In motion pictures, the audience must see everything through the camera's eye. If there is no movement within that area covered by the camera-eye, the story stands still. Movement for the sake of movement is totally unwarranted. Dialogue cannot take the place of movement, and movement cannot replace dialogue. Movement is created by thought and reaction which, in turn, results in meaningful motivation. Dramatization of an idea in movement is the most important aspect of motion and must be applied to the story and the character.

The story line for the screen is usually derived from the dialogue. The less one talks about something, the closer one is to dramatization. Often the most moving and expressive scene is that which contains little or no dialogue. Visually-impressed action expresses a real situation, creating constant audience interest, and arouses a certain expectation and suspense. Visual action, therefore, keeps the audience alive with the story. The use of visual action can be summed up as follows: Things we talk about, we don't have to see—things we see, we shouldn't have to talk about.

In the film medium, it is necessary to project situations in which the visualized emotions are in direct relationship to the dialogue and sound. A well-planned and prepared scene creates an emotional reaction for the audience in direct relationship to the situation on the screen. The structure of dramatization creates audience identification through motion and suspense.

The director selects and arranges his camera angles to tell the story. The correct camera angle highlights the dramatic moment. Every movement of the camera or of the character must have a reason and meaning and be of dramatic value. Movement requires clear and concise motivation.

The choice of angle or shot (long, medium, close or moving) must be considered as a development of story and relate to the desired total effect on the audience. The director works from the master scene which forms a foundation for all shots in the scene. A master scene generally takes in one completely story sequence from beginning to end, without the detailed description which is later expressed in various angles and closer shots. The master scene provides the framework from which all details are developed.

The master scene tells the story, but the interaction and covering shots are those which more fully develop the emotional theme so it can be expressed to and impressed upon the audience. A master scene can begin with and remain in a long shot; or it can begin with the long shot and end in a close-up.

There are no hard and fast rules stating how the master scene must begin or end, but it must establish the prevailing mood and atmosphere.

A DIRECTOR ASSIMILATES

A director prepares for the exact moment which will reveal and impress the story premise and development on the audience. His judgment and interpretation of that moment will make or destroy the total effect of the scene.

A director should remain objective at all times, while at the same time interpreting the contrasts and conflicts of a theme so that the actor is free to apply his own imagination to his role and characterization.

A director should carefully prepare his actors so that the expression of their interpretations supports and clarifies those of the director.

A director should possess a certain insight in order to bring out the inner capabilities of every performer in his story. A director assimilates life in every detail.

There is something in everyone's life that spells out his experience and reactions. Experience is the teacher for the director. He learns by observing and by being aware. He learns by questioning. A director, therefore, looks to others for experience and expression, then looks to himself to answer the following questions:

How much creative sensitivity should I have?

How do my "instincts" react to the problem?

How must I sift the details so as to project the total effect of the story?

What new technical developments can I use to further the projection of the theme and environmental aspects of the story?

How much of a theatre background must I have?

How should I observe life?

How do I listen?

Do I think when I listen?

Do I look for talent?

Do I recognize it?

Do I look for expressive themes?

What is style—my style?

Can I make a decision?

A director distinguishes himself by the methods he uses and by his style to control the visual, audible and emotional elements of the story.

He should have a great interest in the arts and dedicate himself to them. It requires dedicated work to make a film. However, he must be creative. When the story and theme are truly expressed and its characters directed with infinite care, the creative director speaks with the eloquence of a gifted poet with the greatness of a musician with the sensitive artistry of a master painter.

THE QUESTION EVERY DIRECTOR ASKS

What is directing? Many of the great directors themselves have asked the same question. They are forever in pursuit of the answer and are challenged by the question every time they direct a film.

Perhaps the true answer lies only with the audience. And every great director has had the "bitter" and the "sweet" experience to know it.

Countless questions are asked by student and artist. Countless answers are given by the great film makers, who are themselves still students of the theatre. They are constantly seeking new ways to work with and learn the truths of their profession.

"A director must learn how to think with responsibility and truth, for he has the ability to stimulate the thoughts in those with whom he comes in contact. Thinking is a stimulant for ideas", said Director WILLIAM WYLER.

"A director must distinguish truth between what is important to the quality and success of a story and picture and what is not", contended Director HENRY KING. When in Rome, King was told by Cardinal Bonzano, "We are both preachers; but you, Henry, preach to more people in one day than I do in a lifetime. It's a great responsibility, because it's a far greater crime to put one drop of poison in a man's thinking than to put it in his tea."

"Unlike a painting, a poem or a novel, a film is the result of the combined creative efforts of many talents", Director GEORGE SEATON said.

"The director must be a watchdog of believability and guard against any intrusion which might destroy veracity and audience involvement. Direction is a means, not an end in itself."

Director NUNNALLY JOHNSON said, "A director is a feeler of emotions and he must train himself to trust his own reactions. A director is a challenger of thought. A director is an artist, and as an artist he must be willing to learn and learn. Such a process never ends. Every story and presentation is a new experience and a new problem and it cries for a new approach."

Director GEORGE CUKOR related, "When I direct a picture, I do a great deal of research. I absorb myself in the story. After I find the truth, I let my instincts go, for I have learned to recognize that a moment is right when my instincts tell me so."

"It is not enough that a film-maker reflects life through cinemascope but rather through a microscope," said Director RAOUL WALSH.

"When a director develops a story for the screen, he acts in the same way a student learns in school: by absorption. Through absorption, mood can develop for the theme."

Director FRANK CAPRA stated, "A good director never shuts his mind's-eye to the excitement of a new discovery."

"But the story is the thing," proffered Director SAM WOOD.

"A director must learn to be flexible with ideas and theory. His work tends towards constant changes. This moment of improvement can take place at any time: during shooting, before or after."

Director LEO MCCAREY related, "Many times I've decided to change one word, one line, one speech or one scene. The overall effect toward which I strove became totally and completely solidified. The director must train himself to recognize the right moment to do what has to be done, and do it."

"Every story has a new problem. A director directs according to the subject, for it is the subject that dictates how to utilize the method of working," advised Director JOSHUA LOGAN.

"Film making is story making," confided FRED ZINNEMANN.

"I reach to the audience to have them share emotionally in the story. If I cannot reach my audience emotionally, I have failed."

"The director, as an artist, must learn how to execute the theme and the purpose of the film to entertain. A director must learn how to execute to the artists and technicians his positive thinking. His is a business of unwavering decisions. A director must also have the ability to relate the skills and execute his responsibilities with finesse," affirmed director DANIEL MANN.

Director MARK ROBSON believes, "A motion picture director does not have to be a dictator. His urbanity and intelligence are born of an even temperament and vast experience. He finds no need for the domineering theatrics that at one time were synonymous with the word, director."

Director ROBERT WISE said, "My approach to the theme is to discover the objectives of the story's statement to find its totality. Through this search, I am able to discover the action over which I exercise control. The action must not depart from the theme at any time. Such careful examination does not cease during the production. Every single scene and every character must be examined for contrasts, conflict and objectives."

Director CHARLES VIDOR contends, "Direction is a business of intense imagination for each problem may have a different approach; it is as if the experience is first happening."

"It is not a visual problem alone, for the settings, the characters and the story are happenings at the very moment, in time and space," said Director VINCENTE MINELLI.

"The best way to express theory is through the eye of experience. The audience should be involved in the music, words, sounds and effects as if they resemble true life," added VINCENTE MINELLI.

"The director expresses his talent with the camera," director MERVYN LEROY related. "And if used honestly as a story-telling medium it becomes a creative tool of the arts. It makes the audience join with the forces of real people, revealing good and bad, and their human-ness."

"A director must learn how to listen, how to write and how to read. A director who is also a writer has a big edge over his colleagues," spoke director, BILLY WILDER.

"I do think that motion pictures are primarily the director's medium —and God help him if he doesn't establish a true rapport with the writer."

Director VICTOR FLEMING said, "The true artist learns to be humble, and humbleness grows from both failure and success. In the final analysis, the artist also learns that failure is as strong a motivation as success."

Director ERNST LUBITSCH stated about the actor, "It is important to think of the actor as a real human being, for he is, in truth, an integral part of the director. The actor's motivations are more than mere markings on the floor. The actor is not a robot. The director who preconceives an actor's actions cheats both himself and the actor and by so doing restricts the flow of movement within the picture thus helping to dilute the full effect of the theme."

THE DIRECTOR'S INTENTION—To be Creative

Capable direction is based upon creative intention. A picture is dependent upon the imagination and impressions that are intelligible to the eye and ear.

To interpret the life of things with meaning to an audience, the decide what needs to be seen and heard, what has the feeling of decide what needs to be seen and heard, what has the feling of motion in it. Visual discovery lives with the concentration of spirit the director puts into his work.

The director's function is to create reality—within the frame of reference of a story. This demands a hyper-sensitive and disciplined eye, a feeling for relationships, an intuitive proficiency to arrest to the utmost that which the eye perceives. A director must be able to interpret his imagination into a credible form.

The film medium demands this visual sensibility of vision to manipulate reality and illusion into continuous flow and into con-clusion.

A director is a fountainhead of imagination. He controls logic, tact and sensibility. He learns to organize human feelings in dramatic form. He develops poetic vision, a perception into human motiva-tions, a force to deal with. He can deal with film as a medium expressing human emotions. He can put experience into life. A good director is a creative person.

Creativity is a capacity that may be discovered in many human beings, that can be consciously cultivated and developed. A creative person responds to his imagination. He constructs, builds, arranges, and thinks. He rearranges, reconstructs, rebuilds and he continues to think. Further, he responds to resources within himself. He continually enlarges his capacity to deal with and express his thoughts. Every thought is a challenge. Every challenge depends upon a positive decision. Creativity is intention to challenge thought and imagination.

Chapter 3

DRAMA AND THE DIRECTOR

The Needs of the Director
Drama... Story... Actor
...Audience... Technical
Excellence... The Voice of
the Dramatist...

DRAMA AND THE DIRECTOR

The Needs Of The Director

DRAMA .. STORY .. ACTOR .. AUDIENCE
.. TECHNICAL EXCELLENCE ..

The primary intent of "Creative Intention" is to provoke the individual's imagination to respond creatively.

Creative dramatic composition is found by examining, reproducing, and connecting "life" and facts with an objective—the entire creative effort, the film, accepted by an audience.

An artistic performance demands that the performance move forward by building emotions and reactions, and combining the important elements into a total relationship.

THE DRAMA—To Create Illusion

Drama is everywhere. It is discovered and expressed in the tales and actions of human emotions, in reactions and meanings, in struggles, discords, and in the harmonies of experience. Drama is discovered in the many contrasts of life.

The ingredients of drama are many: dialogue, picture, effects, sound and emotions.

The substance of a drama for an audience is the relationship of theme to characterizations, plot, and environment. The drama must be translated into composition which can impress an esthetically expressed idea in terms of an identifiable life-like pattern upon an audience.

The imagination of the dramatist—be it by means of writer, producer, director, artist, technician or editor—is expressed through his interpretation of the logic of life. This interpretation ultimately leads to creative illusion.

Interpretive dramatizations reveal the spirit, uncover the richness of imaginative detail, and set a rhythm of the story to scene and character, thus allowing easy discovery by and for an audience.

Dramatization is putting together the elements of picturization and sound composition to create action and reaction. It is presenting an esthetic composition into theatre for an audience.

THE STORY—Expression of Life

Drama in the story is partially expressed through dialogue which motivates significant action. Such drama contains a theme which, like a thread, is woven throughout the story connecting the beginning, the middle and the end. The spirit of this theme is transmitted by the writer, actor, director and technician to an audience.

Stories with similar themes may follow entirely different routes. The course of their geography depends upon the individual artist's interpretation and point of view.

31

The theatre, stage, motion pictures, television/radio and other processes or devices that technology may invent for a fundamental art are as different as hands, feet, and face, but they are all one body. The difference lies in the method of communication. However, in each case, the story is fundamental.

THE ACTOR—The Interpreter

The actor is basically a theatrical figure. The approach of the actor to the character lies in truthful, artistic expression. He can exist only with a complete surrender of himself to the nature of his objective—to the role he plays.

The audience is drawn into the actor's thoughts and emotions. His thoughts and emotions, therefore, are directed toward control of the audience's reactions. The communication is direct. The actor's face reflects and thereby engages him in psychological rapport with his audience.

THE AUDIENCE—The Responder

The audience is the primary purpose for which a drama exists. Its response to the physical, emotional and audible elements extends the need for creative interpretation of a theme, character, plot, and environment of a story.

The audience for all media can be compared to a "wall of faces" in a theatre of the world. This world-wide audience seeks to be informed and entertained. The ideas, the language and the characters must be so directed that the audience is allowed the pleasure of discovery and enjoyment.

It is not only for knowledge and entertainment that the arts exist, however. Their basic premise is to project a better understanding of all areas of life.

Such projection in the film cannot be an outward one for, unfortunately, the collective universal audience claims it does not desire to be "educated" per se. It does not wish to pay for a "message". It only wishes to be entertained.

An audience is a collection of individuals from all walks of life who have varying interests and associations, yet, collectively, they are considered as "one", and so the film is geared to their total rather than individual reactions.

AUDIENCE INFLUENCE

By the very nature of the motion picture, the audience can virtually be influenced into believing it has ability to attain a feeling of close and intimate contact with the characters, often the actor himself, and with the propounded thesis. Simultaneously, however, the audience realizes that the images being projected on the screen are only images.

With such a basic understanding of audience structure and reactions, the director now more fully understands that every picture with which he is concerned must have meaning and purpose.

The achievement of greatness in film-making is not easy and is not a result of happenstance. It is the outcome of hard work by the dedicated individual who recognizes that within the total film there is and can be complete unity in its final psychological form. Everything in the film must support truth—believability.

ILLUSION OF REALITY

The illusion of reality created by the use of elements of picturization and sound composition is the distinguishing characteristic of the audio-visual media (film). Creation of illusion of reality is the means by which a creative originator secures a response from the audience. The desired audience response comes only when the audience, within the frame of reference of the story, finds the events credible or believable.

If the elements of picturization and sound composition have not been used effectively, the audience will reject the story because what it views is not credible or believable. The originator has failed to create an illusion of reality.

Regardless of the absurdity of a story, the audience will enjoy it or respond if it is presented with the illusion of reality—if it is credible within its own frame of reference, both as a story and as a film interpretation. The illusion may be destroyed at any point by the writer, the director, the actor, the technician or the editor.

LEVELS OF PROJECTION

The nature of the audio-visual media, with its sound and effects, makes possible a clear-cut projection of life. Yet, since it is a form of artistic expression, it is capable of maintaining a level of esthetic scope. The sights, sound and music are combined to achieve a total effect, yet they can remain separate in their own identity and mood. Their inclusion in the story helps to project a greater illusion of life, with its moods and emotions, and by their very placement, create significant emotions with esthetic force. Such a conception of the inherent nature of the art of the audio-visual media is synonymous with the reality of life.

INTIMATE THEATRICAL PROJECTION

One cannot truly say that only the film can achieve a feeling of intimacy. Such intimacy, in varying degrees, can and has been achieved on the legitimate stage.

The existence of any form of theatre depends upon the existence of an audience. Audience interest can be maintained by individual artists, who are dedicated in purpose and who possess the will to create new ideas, themes, and characters which, through projection, will inspire, entertain, instruct and provoke thought.

The question is how? What does the artist need to guide him in achieving such a goal?

He needs sensitivity and spirit plus a method by which he can

conduct an evaluation of that with which he is dealing and those
with whom he is dealing.

Following is a guide to such an evaluation.

(1) *Theme*—is the chosen subject matter of a phase of life that
is universally known?

Do the characters react throughout the story in such a universal,
common-to-all manner that the audience can escape into the life of
the story? Do they have to react in a common-to-all manner to be
believable?

Does the story at the climax bring out some general truth of life,
to establish some conclusive feeling?

(2) *Unity*—Do the same elements appear as a problem in the
opening crisis and in the solution at the climax?

Do these same elements continuously reappear throughout the
story? Do they have to?

Does every action, reaction, and dialogue advance the central
problem?

(3) *Dominant Trait*—Is the introduction of the main actor's dominant trait apparent in the beginning of the story? Does there have
to be a main actor?

Does the main actor's dominant trait manifest itself consistently
throughout the story in his actions and decisions?

Is the climax of the story reached as a result of the main actor's
dominant trait bringing about the final action?

(4) *Desire*—Is the main actor motivated in his efforts by one
single, strong desire from the opening crisis through the story to
the climax? Does it have to be one single desire?

Does the story offer the main actor a definite reward if he wins,
or threatens him with a definite penalty if he loses? Is there always
a need for justification?

(5) *Opening Crisis*—Does the story introduce the main actor's
reaction to some crisis in his life?

Does the story intimately interlock that which has previously hap-
pened with the forward action of the story?

(6) *Single Line of Conflict*—Is every situation presented through
the main actor's eyes? Does it have to be?

Does the author remain objective, excluding himself from every
scene? Why? Should he?

Does the main actor's reaction to the conditions appear pertinent,
dramatic, and significant to him?

Is the story definite in "picturizing" the action from cause to effect,
and reason and meaning so that the audience can see, hear and
sense the drama?

Are the senses attuned to the tempo of pacing the dialogue of the
main character? What about other characters?

(7) *Main Actor*—Is the one main actor dominant, moving through the story in control of each scene? Does he have to be?

Does the main actor renew his intent to achieve his goal enough times to enter the continuous flow of interest about him?

Does the main actor bring about, through his own efforts, the solution of his problem? Is a solution necessary?

(8) *Opposition*—Does the opposition threaten the main actor in the opening scene? If not, when is the main actor threatened?

Does the opposition sustain his efforts through the body and climax of the story?

Does the sinister force of the opposition appear in a hint of disaster?

Does the main actor feel that he is threatened by this hint of disaster? Why?

Is the menace strong enough to jab the audience into immediate concern for the main actor? Is it concern you want?

(9) *Audience Interest*—Does the story begin at the point where the main actor is confronted by a problem that puts the audience in a state of suspense about the outcome?

How much exposition should there be before the story begins?

Does the story open at a point where the main actor realizes that something is wrong? Is it necessary to open the story at this point?

Is there a question in the audience's mind throughout the entire story? In relationship to what?

TECHNICAL EXCELLENCE

The tools of communication are the means for a successful creative endeavor.

In the creative arts there is a definite relationship between the equipment of the artist and his ability to express himself esthetically.

Just as the concert violinist requires a perfectly tuned instrument for performance and the portrait painter, perfectly pigmented oils, which result in full color representation, so the interpreter of the dramatic arts requires proper instruments for true expression of his creative intent.

The use of proper "tools" has a definite purpose in the projection of a visual and audible statement.

The originator must know the tools of his trade. His camera, lenses, lights, microphones, sound elements and tools of scenic design are similar to the musical instruments in an orchestra which, when correctly combined, perform in harmonious composition.

The successful composer knows the capabilities of each instrument and which combinations will be most effective. The dramatic interpreter must be similarly aware of the capability and limitations of his means.

Obviously, the dramatic artist must choose the equipment which is best suited to his needs and which will best aid him in expressing theme, character and environment resulting in a true, sensitive and imaginative product. This ability to select is referred to as technical excellence.

The entire process of visual, audible and emotional communication depends upon proper interpretation of a story through the means of technical excellence.

The drama, the story, the actor and the audience all depend upon the creative application of technical excellence. In the medium where contrasts of expression are necessary, the hand is as important as the mind.

THE VOICE OF THE DRAMATIST—by Arthur Ripley

"Teacher of scholars, servant of students"
The late Arthur Ripley, served for over a half-century in the arts of the theatre as a writer, producer, director, and film editor. As the head of the Motion Picture Division at the University of California, Los Angeles, Professor Ripley established an approach in teaching the student to perform creative work on a professional level.

"A wise man of the church, discussing an approach to religion, once said, "You don't go into religion head first. You must go into it heart rst. The head will follow."

"Consider these words of this wise man for just a moment—that this same simple yet profound approach to religion, applies also to the approach to any of the many forms of the arts.

"The expressed creativity of an individual is an expression of art in its highest form, and it demands of the aspirant an almost religious dedication to this profession before he can hope to achieve it.

"This dedicated approach must be re-enforced with knowledge and truths—we need never relax the tension of our practical efforts and we must teach our minds a new approach to nature. We will then penetrate, by a kind of sympathy, to the real nature of the object, thus discovering for the first time, the strangeness, the multiplicity of its quality.

"Turning our gaze inward we discern the continuity and the freshness of our inner life—of our visions or intuition. Thus, Benedetto Croce, the Italian philosopher, defines art as—vision or intuition.

"Perhaps it could be argued that this definition of art by Croce is too obscure, too undefined for any practical approach to artistic expression. However, consider, too, Croce's brand of intuition: When stimulated by dedicated teaching it perhaps guarantees the transformation of ordinary achievement—achievement charged with reason and high purpose.

"For the student in dramatic arts in such areas as writing and directing, the heart-first approach and the introduction of this kind of high purpose and the nurturing of the inner intuitions is all but indispensable. This moral and spiritual approach to the dramatic arts might not seem to be consistent with the dispensing of soap, but it is entirely consistent with the dedicated aims of an individual who seeks to express art in its highest and creative form.

"We are all at least born with intuition, and I believe that there is an unscheduled ingredient in the spirit of things that can kindle the most ordinary beginner's mind into an unextinguishable flame of intuitive vision. That is why it seems imperative to me that the study of humanities, and their relationships to the fields of drama should be thoroughly indoctrinated in the formative years of teaching and learning.

"The student who has been exposed by an illuminated teacher to the lyrical beauty of Shelly or Keats, or to the wisdom and dauntless courage of a Socrates or in the transcendentalism of an Emerson, or in the profundity of a Spinoza or exposed to the simple child-like faith of an Assisi, is certainly better prepared intellectually to assimilate and understand the value of any technique he undertakes to learn.

"This is the first of three steps that should be taken before a student of drama either attempts the writing of dramatic material or the direction of a script; and certainly before the student of acting attempts to step on a stage or before a camera, to give a performance.

"The second step is a further projection of the first; specifically it is the studies of dramaturgy—the translation of the humanities into dramatic form.

"The third step is when the writer or director becomes aware of the superior position of an audience. He must learn what is meant by an audience transition. The difference between the telling of a story and the dramatizing of one. This becomes an important formula to the student who is seriously approaching the writing and directing profession as a career.

"The true artist never ceases in his dedication to the search for and growth of creative expression."

In his credo, Mr. Ripley seems to say that a classical education is necessary to the successful originator. However, he is actually saying that the successful creator must have developed esthetic insights, awareness, sensitivity and appreciation that one gains from an inspired teaching of the classics. He knew that many possess these qualities who have not known Shelly, Keats or the classics as he refers to them.

❧　　❧　　❧

Chapter 4

STORY PROJECTION FOR THE MEDIA

...A Wall of Faces...Screen Technique...The Elements of a Picture...Means for Projecting Story...Audience Discovery...Actualization of Idea...Scenario Structure...Sight-Suspense-Excitement-Reaction...Adaptation...Production Technique for the Story...What Impels Motivation...Aesthetic Balance...The Trademark of the Artist...Working Demonstrations...

A WALL OF FACES—The Senses Unseen

The audience in the theatre has been called "A Wall of Faces". We may extend this analogy to the other side of the proscenium as well. From the "Wall of Faces", the creative originator must select bodily attitudes in relation to environment or setting to compose visually a picture which communicates situation, plot, theme, character and resolution.

We approach the realization of creative intention—your creative intention, from the standpoint that the story is the beginning, middle and end of an entire creative effort.

ABOUT—THE TITLE—THE ILLUSTRATIONS

For the drawings and illustrations in this book, we have selected bodies from the "Wall of Faces"—faceless bodies—to best illustrate the visual composition within a frame-line reference.

In your examination of this book, examine critically the drawings and illustrations. They were drawn and selected from an interpretation of the text. They have a two-fold purpose: first, to more clearly express what is explained; and secondly, to further stimulate your imagination.

From this critical examination, you may possibly think of a better way in which to illustrate the text. This is good, and this is what we want, so long as you are creating a point of view that is your own.

Once you have established your own point of view, then you must put it to work. This point of view is creative and once put to work, you establish an intention.

SCREEN TECHNIQUE

The story structure of the film has other functions as well as that which projects a story for entertainment alone.

The educational film instructs. The newsreel reports. The documentary conveys information, interpretation and comment. The commercial persuades and sells an idea, product or service.

Story structure for the media is the means by which countless themes and plots are dramatized. The specific structure of the story depends upon the theme of the story as related to the experience of the audience and originator. In analyzing the structure we are not dealing solely with the end-result of the story for the media but also with the whole process that brings the story into being.

Even in a production which has no story in the traditional sense, the originator may appeal to the senses of an audience to elicit a specific response. For example, the "time capsule" technique for presenting a sequence of events can evoke a feeling of overwhelming rapidity of change. A screen filled with constantly changing images accompanied by cacophonic music evokes a feeling of confusion in

an audience. Further, a picture of someone smelling a beautiful
rose with a pleasant expression on his face elicits the audience's
sense of the rose's fragrance. Or, a particularly effective image of a
rough texture makes members of an audience almost "feel" the
texture. The entire story is told in a succession of images following
apparatus involved as the story is projected to be seen and heard.
The use of technological resources, the complex organization of people,
camera and lenses, lights, devices, microphones, and optical effects
all combine to give life to the illusion of reality.

THE FRAMEWORK OF THE FILM ACTION

We begin by developing a scenario form which translates the
essence of the original story, novel, essay, historical events or com-
mentary into the audio-visual medium. Its terminology and arrangement are determined by the technical means by which the actions
in the story will be photographed and communicated to an audience.

The camera, the composition of the photographic image, the microphone, the recording of the words, sounds, picture and effects all
further the principals of unity in terms of transitions and final climax.
This is, in essence, the method of cinematic story telling.

A single photographic image, corresponding to a still photograph,
is called a frame. The pictures move at a specified rate of frames
per second. For example, motion picture film moves at 24 frames
per second: television film, at 32 frames per second. The film is
measured in feet and we speak of footage in discussing the length
of scenes of the whole picture.

The smallest unit of action is the scene, also identified as the "shot"
or "take". The film story progresses with chronologically numbered
preceding and succeeding divisions called sequences. These sequences
are bridged by major breaks in the action known as transitions.

The film is not created within the limits of the proscenium arch of a
theatre, and is not dependent upon the technical resources that are
available backstage. The angle of vision is not determined solely by
the spectator's position in the auditorium, but by an infinite variety
of angles and proportions from which the camera can take in a scene.

The whole story on film has much greater extension in time and
space utilizing a camera-eye technique to move the photographic
images of a novel to be seen instead of read, only the movement is
that of the human mind. The responses to what is seen, heard and
felt are understood.

Dramatization for the media has to be translated into the language
of film action on the screen, where the events must be identified with
people who are either observing the action or participating in it.
The film story, as it takes place, is an instant happening and is in
constant motion.

The devices, cameras, lenses, lights and microphones are capable
of taking in any details of the environment, including people. Consequently, the emphasis which will accurately communicate the story's

meaning must be achieved by selection of appropriate details in audio-visual composition.

In general, the entire social framework of a picture, the characterizations and structure of composition are revealed on the screen, since the camera and microphone can explore the whole system of causes and effects that culminate in the climax of the story.

To create meaningful units of picturization, the originator/interpreter must:

(1) Have an understanding of the mechanics of photography.

(2) Have or develop an individual style in dealing with perspective and a point of view in each unit.

(3) View each unit as related in a consistent eye-to-movement direction. A continuity must be maintained to form a sequence which flows smoothly as it is happening.

(4) Be able to project the meaning of the dialogue in action and reaction.

(5) Have knowledge of audio-visual composition, timing, pacing and rhythm.

(6) Be sensitive to emotion and know how to express it.

The viewer should be made to feel that he is seeing reality. He should never be conscious of the technical process and mechanics used to create the composition.

THE ELEMENTS OF A PICTURE

Following are some of the important elements of composing a picture within a frame-line.

Study carefully the inherent values and characteristics of the following illustrations. Consider the subject, the idea and the event. Determine the primary element.

Interpret and try to improve.

VISUAL SENSITIVITY

Deals with visual communication created by technical means to make the audience not only see but feel. This form of communication is but a means to an end. The end is publication and mechanical reproduction through artistic and perceptive interpretation.

An elderly lady is distressed. She is quite alone. She may be ill or, perhaps, she has just learned of a tragedy.

(a) Visual Sensitivity

ILLUSION . . .

Deals with environment, locale, mood, atmosphere and setting. The effect of illusion may be created and interpreted through perspective. The effect can be more freely expressed through the interpretational placement of the "camera-eye."

In illustration (b) we discover masses of people without actually seeing them.
The effect of "sound" without seeing the source creates implied space and drama.

(b) Illusion

THEME AND IDEA . . .

Deals with emotional experience through reaction. The director should use his power of imagination to express the story in each picture, not only what the camera should take in, but in the emotional quality expressed by the angle.

In the physical setting, we discover a time, a place and motivation to suggest an aspect in the story.

(c) Theme and Idea

EFFECT . . .

Deals with contrasts in environment produced by artistic design which evokes an intended response. An environment may change through the use of lighting and special devices. The change is indicated by the mood of the story.

The light source and silhouette provides a mood for discovery. The single animate object contrasts sharply with its environment.

(d) Effect

POINT OF VIEW . . .

Deals with the details of a visual composition which are selected to communicate a situation, an idea, or an emotion to an audience. Every scene, sequence and transition must have a point-of-view. Selection of details depends; first, upon the director's interpretation of the story; second, upon the actor's interpretation of his role; and third, upon the creative use of nearness, distance, height, depth, size and movement.

In order to capture the visual composition, the originator must be able to select proper angles and lenses to establish perspective and continuity for the completion of every scene, sequence and transition of the film. The audience then sees what the camera sees, after the process of editing the "story footage" has been completed.

Shifting attention can easily be motivated from any point in the triangle to the other.

(e) Point of View

CONTINUITY . . .

Deals with construction, arrangement, and pattern of a picture. The angle must suggest the film effect to be used to create the continuity. Continuity is a development of the film's continuous movement, inner structures of scenes, linkage between scenes, and climax. The system of change is from preceding to succeeding events, time, actions and places.

. . . (f-1) provides orientation for the action to come.

(f-1) Continuity

... **(f-2) Engages and develops the meaning of the action.**

(f-2) Continuity

... **(f-3) Concludes the meaning of the action.**

(f-3) Continuity

TRANSITION . . .

Deals with a process enabling the advancement of the drama to grow out of the story elements. The process advances actions, time, place and the character of the story.

The transition is vital, not only because it ends a scene and sequence and begins another, but because it is, in itself, the essence of the action, changing the meaning of the separate images, time, place and character of the story and provides the force that drives the story forward to conclusion.

Illustration (g-1) and (g-2) in a transition provides one environment, (winter) changing to summer.

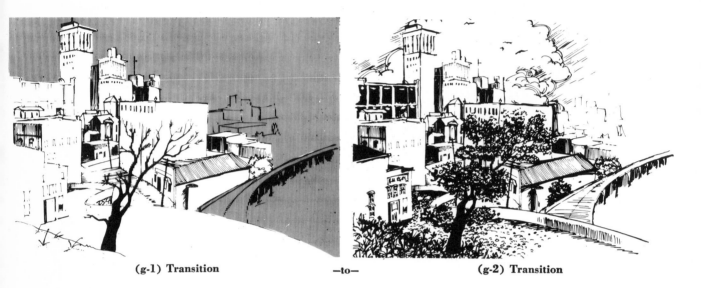

(g-1) Transition   —to—   (g-2) Transition

ATMOSPHERE . . .

Deals with the physical setting that creates a mood. The visual construction of an environment in which the action of a story takes place must support characterization, meaning, mood and interpretation of the story.

Imagination, freedom of thought and idea must be used to establish atmosphere, visually.

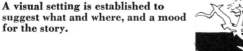

A visual setting is established to suggest what and where, and a mood for the story.

(h) Atmosphere

LIGHT AND SHADOW . . .

Deals with the qualities of mood. Light and shadow define relationships between effect, continuity, people, images and the emotional quality of the environment and setting. It is the responsibility of a director of photography to accept the dictates of a story to use light and shadow imaginatively to create a credible illusion and to direct the eye to detail.

A deep forest containing two adversaries.
Light is used to emphasize the oppositions.
Contrast and conflict provides the mood of the scene.

(i) Light and Shadow

DIMENSION . . .

Deals with space, shape, size, plane, line, balance, variety, stability, sequence, movement and color. Form in the film image has a counterpart in music. In music, the form is aural and depends upon intervals of pitch and time.

In the visual form, the intervals become space, shape, size, plane, line, balance, variety, stability, sequence, movement and color in any combination of pacing and timing.

One factor (soldier with gun) is the focal point.
See this illustration as a cube with all compositional components in it.

(j) Dimension

The stimulating dimension and potential of the film image is limitless. The technical and aesthetic properties created in the film image by the artist are of vital importance and consideration when dealing in cinematic structure to project a story on film. The film image is fundamental to direction.

MEANS FOR PROJECTING STORY

Dramatization can be found in a PICTURE—without speech...

"The deepest wishes of the heart find expression in silent prayer"

In the SOUND without—the picture...

"The 'shot' is heard . . . and the boy knows he'll never ride his horse again . . ."

In the DIALOGUE without—picture or sound...

Dramatization can be found in what we see, and react to—in the form of a story having a BEGINNING—MIDDLE and an END.

AUDIENCE DISCOVERY

Effective dramatization is the method used to allow an audience to discover. The producer of an artistic presentation is constantly searching for new ways to stimulate this audience discovery.

The viewing of cinematic expression can be an experience in reality, an emotional experience resulting from sight and sound. Drama results from a relationship of ideas, feelings and emotions. It exists everywhere.

Every manuscript is the product of a creative imagination. Dramatized realism is not always a factual and exact portrayal of life. The manuscript is a pattern of selected events which can impress upon the audience a discovery of identifiable experience.

The interpretation and projection of the story material can skillfully lead and control audience emotion without allowing it to realize that which separates the world of realism from the world of imagination.

Discovery is that intangible product which excites one's thoughts and preys upon the subconscious motivational drives of an audience. It has the capacity to trigger the subconscious into consciousness.

ACTUALIZATION OF IDEA

The basis of audience interest and control begins with story. The basis of power in the story begins with the idea, which will produce an effect. Effect is found in adaptations of real situations which are then applied to the structure of the film through continuity and transition with picture, sound, and motion.

Dramatization influences the cause and effect of staging reality in the situations of a story. Dramatization is the bringing to life of a story through the development of an idea, with theme, plot, and character.

Dramatization is also achieved by creating suspense. The audience has to wonder what is going to happen. Suspense keeps audience interest alive—the greater the interest, the better the story.

SCENARIO STRUCTURE—Story Structure for the Media

A director must understand the elements of a story, where the focus of attention lies, how and where to place the emphasis. He must understand the emotional attitudes of one character toward another through interpretation of the conflict which brings about reaction.

A thorough knowledge of scenario structure and form is essential to the director.

First, it should help him understand how life is translated into the art form of the film. It should not only illustrate that the scenario is a selection, reorganization, and an intensification of conflict and contrast, but also how conflict and contrast are to be used.

Second, the director who understands story structure will be better equipped to produce the film. He will be able to understand the basic patterns with which the writer works. He can better define the balanced relationship between the characters. He can isolate moments of action and emotional reaction. He can progressively develop, step by step, the various motivations resulting in transition. He can lead an audience to make it see what he wants it to see without driving it to see it. He can control the emotions of an audience.

Third, the most significant thing the director can gain from a knowledge of scenario structure is a recognition of the writer and the director as a working unit in thought and idea. Thought seeks form as water seeks its own level. Form, in the cinematic medium, should be sought by the originator and interpreter.

The first step in the process of creating a dramatic production is the analysis and interpretation of the scenario. The entire pattern of the story should be carefully analyzed for motivational values. The director then analyzes the characters. He determines what motivates their actions and what effects these actions have upon other characters. He traces the development of each character, carefully noting the forces motivating them.

The director must conduct a great deal of research to determine the characteristics of the various personalities in the story, the time, and the environment in which the action takes place. He must determine the theme and select those details which best dramatize the theme.

The story presents a situation. The director, after careful analysis of intention, translates his analysis into visual terms. He confers with the art director, scenic designer, the director of photography, lighting director, costume designer, make-up supervisor, and his production assistants to prepare the scenes as he has interpreted them. The director utilizes all of his imagination to set and block the scenes for the camera so as to emphasize the action for the audience. The action is staged for the camera from a blueprint of the story, which is known as a scenario.

The following is a portion of a story in which the elements serve as the stimulus for ideas. Drama and suspense are inherent in this story action. Because it is read and not seen, the interpretation of it will vary with each reader. The interpreter, however, chooses one point of view which will control the reactions of the audience toward the story.

SIGHT—EXCITEMENT—SUSPENSE—REACTION

A PONY EXPRESS RIDER APPROACHING THE STAGECOACH . . .

The stagecoach traveled about a hundred to a hundred and twenty-five miles a day. The passengers had a consuming desire from the start to see a pony express rider, but somehow all that passed, managed to streak by in the night. The swift phantom rider was gone before anyone could get his head out of the window. (The Exposition)

Every neck was stretched farther. Every eye strained wider. Across the endless dead level of the prairie, a black speck showed against the sky, which kept coming closer. Soon it became a horse and rider, the rising and falling, rising and falling—sweeping toward the stagecoach, nearer and nearer and still nearer until we hear the hoofbeats pounding upon us. (SIGHT—SUSPENSE)

In a little while all interest was taken up in stretching necks, watching for the pony rider.
The fleet messenger who sped across the continent from St. Joe to Sacramento, carrying letters nineteen hundred miles in eight days, suddenly appeared as if from nowhere.
The driver of the stagecoach exclaimed: "He's coming!"

Another instant, a whoop and a hurrah from the upper deck, a wave of the driver's hand, but no reply. (SOUND, EXCITEMENT, REACTION)

. . . and a man and horse rushed past the excited faces like a tail-end of a storm . . .

Both horse and rider went flying by. The rider's dress was thin, and fitted close. He carried no arms—no extras, for even the postage on his literary freight was worth five dollars a letter. (SIGHT)

His horse was stripped of all unnecessary weight, too. He wore a little wafer of a racing saddle and no visible blanket. He wore no shoes. The little flat mail-pockets strapped under the rider's thighs would each hold about the bulk of a child's primer. (SIGHT)

So sudden is it all and so like a flash of unreal fancy that, but for the flake of white foam left quivering and perishing on a mail sack after the vision had flashed by, we might have doubted whether we had seen any actual horse and a rider at all. (REACTION)

ADAPTATION—Ingredients of a Scenario

THEME . . .

A theme is a way of life and can be found in a composition of life's experiences. The theme is an expression of the universal conflicts, drives and emotions of man which motivate him. It is further, a specific statement expressing the universal in terms of the specific story or scenario.

Regarding the theme, the point of view discovered by the audience depends entirely on the originator's interpretation. The theme is, therefore, flexible and can be stylized.

CHARACTER . . .

When there is no conflict there is no drama.

Conflict is one of the elements of drama. Human nature contains conflict, whether it be physical or emotional.

Consider then, that the characters drive the plot and the plot drives the characters.

Individuals are often explained by such words as:

"Distinctive" — "Dominant" — "Peculiar" — "Complex" — "Personal" — "Insecure" — "Bold" — "Frustrated" — "Fearless" — "Romantic" — "Adventurous" — "Lovable" — "Fearful" — "Naive" — "Powerful" — "Energetic" — "Despondent" — "Overpowering" — "Charming" — "Beautiful" — "Lovely" — "Ugly" — "Ill-tempered".

PLOT . . .

The plot is the blueprint of action of a story and is often explained by such as: "Plan" — "Strategy" — "Invention" — "Conspiring" — "Devising" — "Deceiving" — "Twisting" — "Scheming" — "Arranging" something of a developing substance.

Character and plot are developed together. One cannot be divorced from the other. The audience is drawn into the experience and circumstances of the character as well as into the plot. Plot makes apparent the dramatic interest, effect, and style, and it plants the significance of the action of the story.

Too little plot results in a story that does not move, that is static and uninteresting. Too much plot reveals the lack of story and character development that tends to destroy the sensitivity and the elements supporting the theme. The plot must be controlled in the structure of the story.

The framework of action is taken from the fundamental elements found in human emotions. The action exists for the sake of the character and is a direct result of the plot. The audience should discover both the character and the plot.

An audience should not be allowed to anticipate the obvious—but rather the interest circumventing the obvious. Thus the plot and the character cannot live apart. The audience interest lies not only in what is happening but also in what is going to happen. A character in the plot is a likeness of a person who has some identity and is involved in emotional and spiritual conflict.

The author's primary objective is to transfer from life to story a moving portrayal of some aspect or phase of life. This is partially accomplished through full characterization. The principal character should always be discovered by the audience. The audience's reaction becomes the focal point of the story.

ENVIRONMENT . . .

Environment is the home of the plot, the character, and the theme and can be created in the minds of the audience by "clues" given by the actors through the dialogue in the story.

Environment can be found in the action as we create mood, accents and thoughts in the story. Environment is in the physical elements. Environment lies in the atmosphere, which can be simulated by light and shadow. Environment is in the natural backgrounds, or in settings created from realistic backgrounds.

The components in the environment must have visual detail to qualify source. The control of light is governed by source whether it be sunlight, lamplight, candlelight, firelight, or darkness and many and varied weather conditions.

PRODUCTION TECHNIQUES FOR THE STORY

Techniques of production serve as a means to a creative end. The story treatment should be so prepared that the director and artist can project visually and audibly the emotional elements and their motivations, clearly and vividly.

Techniques in production aim towards effective presentation of a story through sight and sound. The parts, acts, scenes, sequences and divisions of a story must contain theme, characterization, plot and environment staged in their proper succession to advance to a climax.

ELEMENTS OF PRODUCTION

The following elements of production are carried out by various production techniques.

(1) *Picturization*—The expression of the creative urge into a visual experience can be accomplished with a camera. The camera is the eye to story liaison between the director and the audience.

All plans evolving from ideas are developed by imagination, designed, and then captured by the camera and microphone and transferred to film.

When a director interprets for the camera, he imagines the action as the audience will see it. He uses his power of selection to express the story in the most moving and effective composition.

The actor may move to the camera, or the camera may move to the actor. The story is the constant context of every frame of film.

(2) *Sound Composition*—Sound complements the picture synchronized to it.

(3) *Dialogue*—The dialogue expresses characterization in the story and helps develop the theme, plot, and the environment.

(4) *Timing*—Timing is the process of changing actions and emotions as the story advances. The director plans the movement of the actors and the composition of the pictures.

(5) *Editing*—implies *Inter-Cutting* parts of footage, (scenes and parts of scenes) provided for the film editor. This is a process of bringing forth the significant points of the story. Inter-cutting allows the adventures of the characters in different places to be inter-related, as the story unfolds. Inter-cutting can sustain suspense.

The sequence of "shots" or parts, must have continuity of action which precedes and follows the complete development of the sequences, one into another, until the final climax is resolved.

Story projection for the media demands artistic technique by all the artists who interpret the drama. The director must strive for clarity and detail.

Each part in the film production is the height of information—the sound can be the fulfillment of what the eye sees. All the approaches to production techniques demand creative intention of the artist. The execution of creative intention must be carried out by a team effort.

THE "PROFESSIONAL" FILM PRODUCTION TEAM

(1) *The Producer*—Is responsible for matters of production and finance. He estimates costs, plans the budget, and acquires the writers, director, actors and chief technicians.

The acquisition of a story idea, from its conception through final marketing, is his primary responsibility.

(2) *The Writer*—Is the first member of the creative team formed by the producer. This creative individual must form and adapt his material so that it is consistent with the requirements of film techniques.

The adaptation consists of a synopsis of each sequence, including the main speeches. From the synopsis the writer or adapter develops the scenario, or shooting script, i.e., detailed breakdown of everything that happens in each scene and sequence including transitions, dialogue sound and effects and main camera movements.

(3) *The Director*—The producer organizes the picture; the director creates it.

(4) *The Cast*—In selecting the cast, producers and directors compromise in order to assemble a company which has both box-office appeal and genuine talent.

Because of the special features of film production, (the many short scenes, the disconnected style of camera shooting, and the tremendous intimacy) the employed acting techniques place tremendous demands upon the actor—demands not found on the stage, or in live radio or television.

The most highly-prized actors are those who can easily project the required emotion for any shot, thus binding together the separate shots which result in one consistent characterization.

(5) *The Cameraman*—is responsible for the physical appearance of the picture. He directs the corps of men who place or move the camera and arranges the placement of lights.

The cameraman, known also as the director of photography, works closely with the director. He interprets the picture in terms of light, shadow, and composition which express the director's feeling for the mood and atmosphere of each shot.

Before the cameraman shoots the scene, three key men have coordinated their creative efforts to bring the picture up to that point: The writer, the producer and the director.

(6) *The Sound Recordist*—The chief sound recordist and his crew of assistants work closely on the set with the director and the cameraman. Aside from making certain each line of dialogue is picked up by his microphones, he directs the movements of the microphone boom and listens for any acoustical flaw or deficiency during the recording of a scene.

After the shooting of a scene, the sound recordist may supervise re-recording, dubbing and transfer sessions.

(7) *The Set Designers*—A producing organization should have a staff of highly skilled craftsmen who can provide settings and properties for any historic period or place required. These are the set designers.

The settings must be reasonably authentic, highly atmospheric in mood, and constructed for optimum sound and camera movement.

The set designers, working with the director, draw sketches and blueprints for each interior as well as each exterior as they will appear in the picture.

Generally, before any actual construction begins, the set designers will prepare scale models of the settings for study by the director and the cameraman. From these models, the director plots the camera angles and movement of the camera.

Designing a setting in the environment of a story in the film media is a highly specialized and complex profession. There is a great deal of cinematic technique involved to create the illusion and/or reality for the particular production.

Creating a visual composition, a pattern for the movement of the camera, the sound perspective and an effective design to enhance the mood depends upon the artists' interpretation of the story.

(8) *The Film Editor*—Inasmuch as motion pictures are an assemblage of hundreds of brief shots, the arrangement of these shots into a smooth-flowing, rhythmic whole is a specialized art. This arrangement is the function of the film editor, who, in turn, supervises teams of specialists in the cutting and editing of sound tracks, effects, negatives, inter-positives, fine-grains, re-recordings, transfers and many sundry items relating to editing the film footage. A good editor possesses a highly developed sense of timing.

He has a keen dramatic sense, knowing how and when to emphasize a scene with a close-up, when to choose the more neutral long shot, and how to sustain audience interest by variation of angles and distances.

The film editor is an architect of story.

(9) *The Composer, Conductor and Arranger*—Every large producing organization uses composers, arrangers, and musical conductors.
In addition, composers from outside the industry are often invited to
provide "scores".

The composer's main purpose is to provide appropriate music for
the various scenes in a picture. The music then, must contribute to
the emotional tone of the scene, and subsequently to the entire
production.

Generally the composer of a film score is permitted to conduct the
recording sessions of his work. However, this function can be and
sometimes is performed by the staff musical director.

The conductor standing before the orchestra faces a screen on
which is projected those sequences requiring music. Through ear-
phones he hears both the dialogue and the sound of his orchestra as
they are blended and recorded.

The working prints, from which he works, have visual cue marks
which indicate the beginning and the ending of each musical passage.

(10) *Technicians*—There is a host of technicians who work at the
direction of the major personnel just listed.

For instance, Unit managers, Assistant directors, Script supervisors,
Art directors, Assistant cameramen, Still photographers, Key grips,
Key property men, Lighting personnel, Light director (gaffer), Effect
cameramen, Set designers, Sound effects, Music effects, Music editors,
Sound boom operators and mixers, Laboratory technicians and "best"
boys.

All of the above mentioned professional production personnel are
members of a craft union and have a scale pay arrangement fixed
for their individual craft. They may be chosen for the production,
assigned on a daily job basis or staffed by a producing company.

WHAT IMPELS MOTIVATION—When the Idea Moves

Drama lives by action. Action supports the character. Any form
of artistic presentation adapted for film is impossible without emotional
and physical action.

Even more important than the action itself are the reasons for
the action and the force and meaning behind it. It must be dramatic
and believable. It must be motivated.

Motivation then, is the reason for the action in a story. Since every
action has motivation, it becomes a cause and effect relationship which
drives the action to its climax.

WHERE TO BEGIN . . .

The beginning lies in the process of interpretation.

First, we must know the needs and significance of the theme in the
story. The actions and reactions to that which is significant lie in the
core of every drama. This is where the director's physical work
begins: the staging of the scenes and sequences.

The product of a scene must show the significance of the action from cause to effect, create and motivate the unity of the action, the unity of time and the unity of place. The unity of action requires that no situations, characters, time, or atmosphere and environments be introduced which are inconsistent with the central theme or mood of the story.

After careful analysis, the story emphasis may be placed and exaggerated in any manner, by the director, only so far as motivation for the action is allowed. The motivations, resulting from the staging, must be clear to the characters and through them to the audience at all times.

WHERE TO CHANGE...

The changes and contrasts in action, and the point-of-view of every action, can be effective only if the director knows WHAT, WHEN, WHY, and HOW.

Motivation is the sum total of the reasons that cause reaction and response. It must be constantly considered in the acceleration, rhythm, tempo and pace in the continuity as the story advances.

Motivation can be expressed in both negative and positive forms. It stems from ideas and purpose. It is derived from decisions, drives, spirit, passions, and frustrations. It is also derived from the will or a desire.

WHERE TO END...

The director will find the motivational forces only after he explores the reasons for the characters' existence. This existence is expressed by the theme of the story from its beginning, through the climax.

ESTHETIC BALANCE—How it can be achieved in composing scenes.

Composing action is interpretation of thought. The problem of cause and effect involves physical movement which is seen, but may be in the hearing or feeling of it.

All actions carry emotional impact which become a developing story factor.

SELECTION...

The director must be selective and specific with regard to what is important in the emotional values, so that the actor can have the opportunity to express the proper motivation.

The blocking of action is a process of selection. The essential values must have significance in what is included, left out or implied.

The physical placement of the characters in relation to each other and establishment of a point-of-view are major considerations.

The director's thoughts must be reflected in the precise selection of details. His selection of details determines his style. The experience and expression of the director will determine which detail he will select to portray an emotion. In turn, this selection of one detail, in preference to another, will identify the style whereby he interprets a story.

Selection is the process of developing and reworking the material of experience. To the writer it means an expression of his imagination. To the director it means to be able to select the dominant avenues which make it possible to expose idea and theme to an audience.

STYLE . . .

Style may be known as that quality which identifies a director, whether he directs adventure, romance, mystery, history, comedy, farce, or real life.

Style may be found in the skillful arrangement of the story and the manner in which it is interpreted. For example, the story may call for a portrayal of fear. Fear may be expressed through a complete paralysis. It may also be portrayed through excessive action or nervous mannerisms.

Style may call for wide areas, small passages or contrasts in the many varied forms of the dramatization.

THE TRADEMARK OF THE ARTIST

Every artist has a conscious or subconscious style which is expressed throughout his work as he achieves his objective.

The many opportunities afforded in film making allow the artist to project this style through creative selectivity to an audience comprised of a cross-section of the world.

The arrangements of artistic creative thinking, which express the trademark of the artist, fall into a variety of general categories; some tend to be bold, crude and obvious, others are subtle, refined and restrained.

Through individual style the artist may, at times, force an audience to participate only in the mechanical or physical features of his presentation. By so doing, this in effect creates an invisible force or screen which allows passage of only the physical aspects rather than the emotional aspects. Whether such style is acceptable or not, the decision lies with the audience.

Whatever style is developed, the artist must consider all aspects of audience reaction, even though the audience is not style's determining factor. Style emerges from a director's consistent desire and individual attempt to express a story from his own inherent point-of-view. Often he is not able to recognize his own style as such, because it emerges through and reflects his attitude toward life itself.

The style of an artist can also be traced to the way he works with people, an environment and the written word. It results in a special emphasis or quality.

Style, then, is found in the development of expression which becomes identified with an individual. It is a creative technique. It is an unique sensitivity to the simple and complex.

Creative style involves the skillful use of every technical means available to make an audience aware of and react to the theme of a story.

Style lies in the invention of expressing one's creative thoughts through a physical and emotional element. It is conceived and nurtured in the mind and expressed through ideas and design. It is characterized by a dominant trait which impels a certain kind of interpretation that is clearly defined in the creative effort of the individual.

Style, then, is an emergence of an individual's characteristic nature expressed in a work of art.

SUGGESTED WORKING DEMONSTRATIONS—For Individual and Group Evaluation

A director's judge and jury are his audience. Their verdict will determine whether he has the means for projecting story, an understanding of motivation, a richness of imagination, style, mood, spirit, the ability to obtain performance from the actor, and a complete knowledge of mechanics.

Choose a scene from the following and work out a pattern of individual style.

a. An elderly couple part after three years of their marriage.

b. A prison cell in death row.

c. A young man arrives at the grave of a person he dearly loved. He did not attend the funeral. This is the first time he has made contact after death.

d. A son says goodbye to his parents as they leave their house to enter a home for the aged.

e. A man is no longer welcome in his brother's home.

f. Two brothers greeting each other after a long separation. Both had parted angrily.

g. A spinster forced to retire, leaves the job she has held for many years.

h. Two sisters say goodbye to each other. One just married the other's fiancé.

i. The setting is a moving elevator in an office building. The only occupants are the operator and a female passenger. The elevator stalls between floors due to a power failure. The lights go out. The passenger has claustrophobia. The operator has recently been released from an institution.

j. A son comes home after a long absence. He has been out of the country serving in the army. The son presents his new bride to his parents. She is much older than he. She is of a different religion and race. She has been married before and has her small 3 year year old child with her.

❀   ❀   ❀

Chapter 5

VISUAL ELEMENTS

Basic Idea Alignment to Visual
Form... Composition...
Dramatic Use of Composition...
Working Demonstrations...
Illustrations...

VISUAL ELEMENTS

BASIC IDEA ALIGNMENT TO VISUAL FORM—The Aspect Ratio
and Screen Composition

The three by four aspect ratio of the audio-visual screen is not an accidental choice of proportion. The wide screen aspect ratio is three to seven, yet it, too, conforms to the same basic rules of composition as the smaller screen.

The screen area is still rectangular and wider than it is tall.

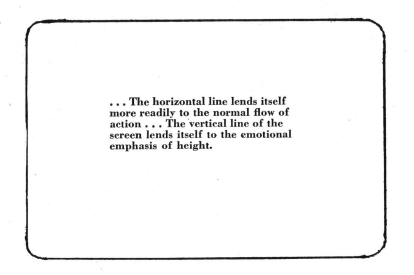

... The horizontal line lends itself more readily to the normal flow of action ... The vertical line of the screen lends itself to the emotional emphasis of height.

THE SCREEN

The horizontal and vertical lines within the frame-line are used:

(1) To emphasize the idea in the area which the lens takes in.

(2) To eliminate an unwanted portion of the picture.

(3) To show and bring forth exact detail in all areas.

(4) To adjust the composition so it becomes an integral part of the story.

(5) To establish a reference point and to determine the exact size of the subject or object.

(6) To take in a field of action within a proscenium area.

Picture composition is considered to be that which is contained within the frame-line and which supports the mood, atmosphere, theme, plot, and characterization of the story. It is primarily achieved by converting ideas from words into visual terms.

Visual composition should combine as many elements of the basic idea as can be used in one dramatic, story-telling scene. The composed scene should express the story motivations allowing the story to flow smoothly from one scene to the next until it reaches its logical conclusion.

The visual content, independent of sound and dialogue, should create the mood of the story. Establishing a point of view and showing a movement of objects in relation to an environment add to the force of a scene and help express the thoughts behind it.

For the scene to carry greatest impact, it is sometimes desirable to distort or exaggerate the perspective. The director's interpretation can be accepted in its distortion as a creative representation of the scene. However, the director should remember that such exaggerations and distortions must be under his control at all times. To do this successfully demands all his dramatic perception and ability.

COMPOSITION

Every picture composition should be carefully imagined and studied in a variety of ways before the actual arrangement is physically composed. The director must strive to arrange the subject and the material in such a manner that it be intelligible in establishment, perspective, and in the meaning of the preceding and succeeding motivations.

In order to express or communicate an idea, the director must compose the picture or series of pictures in such a way that the viewer perceives the image vividly—that he is "impressed" with the idea the director wishes to communicate.

The director needs to organize his composition, ostensibly in the arrangement of the people and object to be meaningful and to support the theme. In this way the emotional elements and the sound elements are consistent with the visual elements. The director must think in terms of visual images which will produce pictures of impact. The successful use of a staging area must be planned with attention to what needs to be stated and what left out.

The artist, as the interpreter, must learn and understand the elements which control his medium in order to create an effective illusion. Unless this exists there cannot be a theatre presentation, and without which the artist is not an artist—he is only a worker.

The director works as an artist to compose a composition. He creates as he works.

PHILOSOPHY OF CONSTRUCTION . . .

Photographic composition is that which is contained within the frame-line of the audio-visual screen. It is simply defined as "being right" for the over-all effect, and relates to the juxtaposition of all scenes.

Composition expressed by the creative artist comes from ideas, which, as guiding forces, are transposed, interrelated and esthetically seen, heard and felt. The most important point to remember about composition is that it should focus the story on people in action, rather than on people who only talk about the action.

The director must remember that his arrangement of ideas in his picture composition is based upon emotional experiences which reflect the feelings and moods of his characters. The audience's reflection upon the characters and their actions allows it to evaluate the terms of its own experiences.

Effective visual composition can be achieved only if the director constructs his compositions to allow the emotional, visual and audible elements to speak for themselves. These elements must be allied so they reach an apex of meaning in each scene and sequence.

Composition is the visual language of the director. Its arrangement is as important as the motivations of the characters. Therefore, every movement within the composition must have meaning. The picture the director arranges must communicate to the audience specific information and create audience participation in every scene.

SCENE OBJECTIVE . . .

The objective of a scene is the purpose of a scene. How does the scene further the plot, characterization, mood and theme of the story? How does it fulfill its purpose or objective?

The scene objective is primarily a story structure problem. The way in which the objective is fulfilled is a composition and staging solution.

The relationship of story and character, both physical and emotional, the actions and reactions, and the motivational forces of the characters and scenes must be completely analyzed in order to clearly define the dramatic objective. Such definition results in an impelling force which can engulf the audience and guide its emotions toward an understanding of the theme. Every part of every scene, by itself, must contain dramatic elements which support the total effect of the story.

The audience is not involved with the mechanics of the scene. It is not associated with their preparation or their technical requirements. It is detached from the production, other than the projection of ideas by which it can evaluate the total effect and the effort of the director's creation.

COMPOSITION AND THE ARTIST . . .

The artist in the film medium is a composer much the same as the artist in music, for composing is nothing less than a collection of parts into a whole. The actor forms a character from a combination of experiences and imaginings; the musician combines notes of music with experience and emotion. The director combines the talents of the actors and technicians, and the director of photography applies knowledge with experience, imagination and emotion to create a defined and controlled composition.

The writer, through a combination of word images, provides the stimulus for the director, actor and technicians.

The director must always remember that visual composition is an instantaneous means of story communication to the audience. Picture elements have many objective and subjective contrasts. The reactions of the audience are controlled by the performed ideas, previous associations, backgrounds and prejudices. The organization of visual material should be characterized by logic and directness, and arranged so that it can flow in an orderly and unobtrusive manner to the audience.

COMPOSITION AND THE EMOTIONS . . .

Composition results from a careful analysis of the various motivational forces contained within the desired overall effect dictated by the theme of the story.

Composition is, therefore, not only physical but emotional. The physical aspects of composition are controlled and suggested by the emotional impressions created by thought and action. Through the method of combining such emotional impressions with the outward physical expressions, a force is thus created which cannot be changed by audience interpretation.

The ultimate goal of creative composition is emotional control, whether expressed by an actor or actors, a director, a writer or a director of photography.

COMPOSITION AND IDEAS . . .

Composition begins with an idea which for the most part is an inward reproduction of past experience coupled with a present concept.

The idea is a trigger for spontaneous action which sets up a train of images. It is the direct responsibility of both the director and director of photography to apply such images or ideas to the creation of a composition which, in turn, will trigger a train of images in the mind's eye of the audience.

PHYSICAL ASPECTS OF COMPOSITION . . .

After an analytical approach to the story, it is most generally acceptable to prepare the story in a visual form known as the "story board".

THE STORY BOARD "THE CHASE"

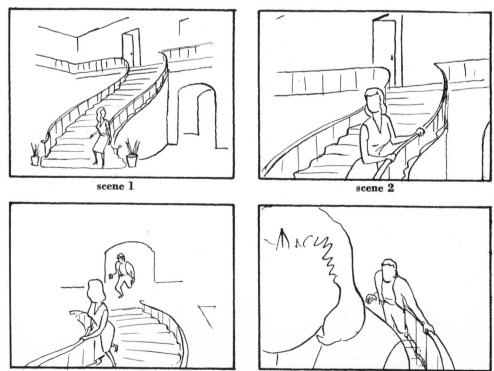

scene 1   scene 2

scene 3   scene 4

The story board is a device which tells the story through illustrations drawn in perspective. Such are the physical aspects of composition. Through the story board technique, the director can visualize the effect, relationship and impact of every large and small physical object within the scene which bears direct relationship to the continuity of the story.

Each point of view, close or far, is examined for its expression of the growth and fulfillment of each scene. The interpretive artist now has at his disposal a method by which he can objectively examine his own interpretation. He will find that within the pattern of a scene, expressed in story board form, that the CLOSE-UP on an object or an individual, contains more movement than the LONG-SHOT.

Such movement therefore cannot be classified as physical dexterity. Rather, it becomes the movement and force of thought, reaction, and idea.

THE FRAME-LINE—DIRECTOR'S PROSCENIUM . . .

The frame-line in the field of a picture, consists of the vertical and horizontal range of vision given to a part of the perspective which results in what the eye sees.

Like a window, as in the illustration, the frame-line directs the emphasis and human-eye interest to the horse and rider, without eliminating any of the other emotional and physical elements.

The frame-line, a window to story

The "frame" in cinematic technique is a reference boundary. The form of the boundary itself is a three by four aspect ratio which can be expanded or reduced, extended or closed-in, placed in a setting or in a natural environment, and seen through the lenses of a camera. The action, so arranged within the frame, appears on a 360-degree, horizontal stage which becomes the field of action for performing the elements of a story.

The position and relative size of the images within the frame-line is important, for their juxtaposition gives emotional value to the eye as it sees, to the ear as it hears and to the mind as it reacts.

The selected boundary "frames in" a field of what is to be seen, left out and implied.

THE STORY IN A PICTURE . . .

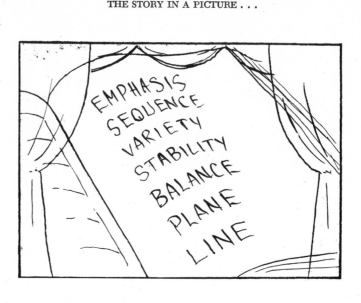

Visual composition, then, is the process of putting together the values of a theme, considering:

(1) emphasis,   (2) seqeunce,   (3) **variety,**

(4) stability,   (5) balance,   (6) **plane,**

(7) line

Composition, as interpreted from the story, reflects thought and action obtained by the use of these visual elements so that they communicate a meaningful relationship of the whole.

This chapter has dealt with the importance of the director selecting emotional and physical values to emphasize the theme, relating the character to the environment and focusing attention on other images in the story.

It is well to remember that every significant structure must have an opposing element that employs a proper balance and contrast to develop from the action itself, the audience attention and interest. Focus on action, from cause to effect, should be organized so that the attention goes directly, easily and quickly to the emphasis of a scene. This is determined by emphatic visual relationships, sound and speech, and the motivation as a result of the relationships.

DRAMATIC USE OF COMPOSITION—Composition Elements

Composition is an arrangement of the elements of a picture and a dramatic relationship in order to interpret a story for the audience.

The groundwork of dramatic style and means of expression for the director lies in the following fundamental principles, which are used to convey the emotional and intellectual values of a drama. Each presentation applies these values to a varying degree and in differing combinations according to the dictates of the story.

Each scene must contain in its composition, at least a part of each of the following:

EMPHASIS

SEQUENCE

VARIETY

STABILITY

BALANCE

PLANE

LINE

These elements are the fundamental principles used in setting the images, the theme and situation into a form and order, enabling the director to stage, interpret, block out a scene and properly motivate the visual, audible and emotional action.

The form of the visual composition is determined by the significance of value and force and in that area where the dramatic action takes place. By proper use of composition, the attention is drawn to the physical and/or the emotional impression in that framed field of action.

The field is, in short, the stage of the scene "framed-in", which appears to the audience, and is known as the frame of action.

The director composes his composition within a frame of reference utilizing the above values to create his picture.

1. EMPHASIS . . .

A director needs to consider the object of attention in his field of action. In a sense the geography of the action itself must have a reason and meaning. The director must think of the composition concerning the arrangement of the elements in the frame-line in such a way that the viewer's eye is immediately drawn to the object of attention.

In illustration (1), the woman on the witness stand is the focus of attention of all present in the courtroom.

(1) Emphasis—Focus of Attention

The focus of attention is achieved by:

Space, Actual Line, Stability, Visual Line, and could be further emphasized by Light and Shadow.

Emphasis is the focus of attention upon a particular element of a picture. Since a story unfolds through its series of attentions, emphasis becomes the most important aspect of composition. It may be obtained through the relationship of the emphatic element to the other elements in the picture.

Emphasis is the most demanding value in every frame as the director composes the action of the story. It is also the principal factor in the continuity of the story.

Emphasis in value serves emotional and physical attention, and it includes:

Actual Line Emphasis, Visual Line Emphasis, Apex, Space, Light and Shadow, and Contrast.

Following are illustrations in which the values are indicated.

(a) Actual Line in EMPHASIS is the line the spectator's eye travels as a result of appropriate arrangement of the picture elements.

In illustration (a), the focus of attention is upon the General in the background.

The rows of converging figures emphasize the principal character on the review stand.

(a) Actual Line Emphasis

In illustration (b), the character entering the room becomes the important point of emphasis because of the visual attention of all the others in the setting.

(b) Visual Line Emphasis

(b) Visual Line in EMPHASIS is the line of attention the spectator's eye travels as it follows the direction in which a character looks.

(c) The APEX position in Emphasis

(d) Emphasis by SPACE

(e) Emphasis by Light and Shadow

(f) Emphasis by CONTRAST

Emphasis can be achieved by the *apex* in which the actual line of attention is formed by the arrangement of the figures and their attention to each other. The emphatic figure is placed at the apex position. In illustration (c), to the left, any two of the three figures can shift their attention to the other one by turning their bodies or vision to him.

Space can serve in the emphasis of attention by the relative proximity of, or distance between, elements of a picture. It may be evidenced in variation of level, dimension, size and perspective. Illustration (d) right, shows the two figures projecting their attention to the third figure who is emphasized or set apart by space.

Light and Shadow captures the emotional quality and provides significance to the definition or obscurence of picture elements. The character in the center, illustrated in (e), left, maintains emphasis because of his position in the light. The shadow around him creates the mood of the theme. He is also emphasized by the visual and actual line in the apex.

Contrast is derived from a break in the spectator's visual expectation. It provides for reflection and tempo in a scene. The characters in illustration (f), right, share their emphasis, each in contrast to the other, because of their position, light and shadow, space and apex.

2. SEQUENCE . . .

SEQUENCE is the arrangement of pictures, one after another, in a logical continuous order to develop the continuity in action and theme.

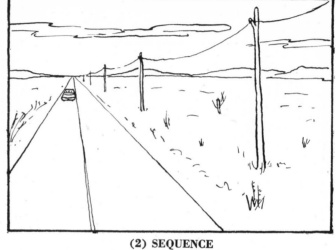

The master scene in illustration (2), establishes the setting for the theme which is to develop. The time is day. The locale is a desolate stretch of highway. The mood is lonely. The moving image in the composition will emerge as the significant beginning. It is a car, moving head-on, which passes out of view at the bottom of the frame.

(2) SEQUENCE

SEQUENCE concerns the progression from one picture to the next in continuity of motion, sight, idea, mood, pace, atmosphere and locale.

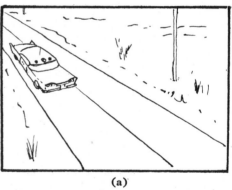

The cars appears immediately from the left, moving right. The angle now is closer to the spectator. Identified is the same locale and highway. The situation heightens in expectancy as we identify the vehicle, a police patrol car moving fast, passing out of the frame.

(a)

The very next frame draws the eye into a closer view of the situation. The tempo is now increased as the same car, moving faster on the same highway, in background, passes out of the same scene, right.

(b)

The scene now appears head-on and we view the police car approaching an accident on the highway. The situation and sequence have now advanced to a breaking point or into conclusion.

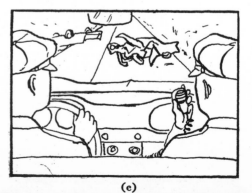

(c)

3. VARIETY . . .

VARIETY is for reflection and pace. Variety offers a change in area, setting, time, character, size, levels, perspective, in all visual elements, in the same theme, to intensify attention and to sustain the interest of the audience.

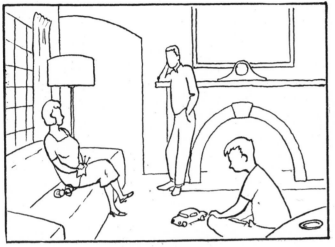

(3) VARIETY

The master scene here shows a man, woman and a boy in the environment of their home. The background reveals a balanced arrangement of the figures, which lends itself to freedom in the use of perspective.

(a) Viewing the woman from the other characters' point of view.

(b) Viewing the man from the other characters' point of view.

(c) Looking at the boy from the man's and woman's point of view.

(d) Viewing the whole scene from another angle with a different focus of attention.

4. STABILITY . . .

STABILITY is the emergence of meaningful parts. Stability is the element of a picture which confines and defines the area, locale, exterior or interior, night or day, mood or atmosphere, in which the action takes place.

In illustration (4), there is **no** question as to the spectator's orientation. The place, locale and time of day are obvious; even the season may be revealed by the foliage or by the color of the countryside and atmosphere. The figures near the haystack, demanding to be viewed up close, are the stabilizing factor which motivates interest and calls for a change of view.

(4) STABILITY

Stability provides orientation for the audience concerning setting, its place and significance in the story.

In illustration (a), the theme develops as we see the figures up close and take an interest in their action.

(a)

STABILITY is the tying down and projection of the position and significance of the important aspect of a scene. The heart of a scene may be supported by other elements, yet stability is the controlling element for proper timing, pace and tempo, projecting that which you want the audience to see, hear and feel.

5. BALANCE . . .

BALANCE is the arrangement of the elements of a picture in such a way that gives value and meaning to the object of attention.

(5) BALANCE

The figures in illustration (5), appear heavily weighted behind the table. However, their visual attention gives emphasis to a counteracting image of interest which balances the composition, making it pleasing to the eye and giving meaning to the theme. The scene is further balanced by dimension and perspective; stabilizing or story telling objects on the walls, the figures in the center and an image of interest in the foreground.

BALANCE also aids in the clear definition of the object of attention in a manner pleasing to the viewer. For example, if the background is not clearly defined, it has no meaning and the audience is not esthetically satisfied with the picture composition.

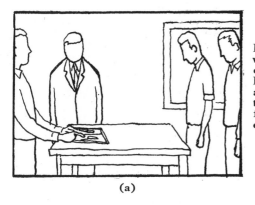

(a)

Illustration (a), shows only a weak two-dimensional balance from one side of the frame to the other. Depth and balance in perspective are lost by the flat, bare wall behind, the awkwardly spaced, static figures, and the lack of actual line emphasis.

In this uninteresting composition, a disturbing break, as the eye travels, replaces the pleasing curve in the previous design.

6. PLANE . . .

PLANE is the dimensional aspect of picture composition. It involves consideration not only of the height and width represented by perspective and size, but it also involves consideration of the angle at which a scene is viewed.

(6) PLANE—What the eye sees

Perspective concerns the appearance of objects in respect to their relative distance, meaning and position.

(a) Height   **(b) Depth**

PLANE is exemplified in illustrations (a), and (b), by a variety of compositions of the same subject showing how the director, in blocking a scene, may select the porportion, dimension and angle which best tells the story.

SIZE is determined by the significance of the emotional or pictorial scale.

Size is what the eye sees, including an emotional reaction to that quality of a thing which determines how much space it appears to occupy.

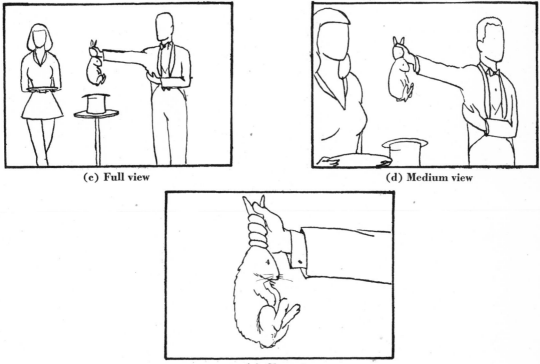

(c) Full view   **(d) Medium view**

(e) Close view

The ANGLE from which a scene is viewed should be selected to achieve proper picture proportion and the perspective dictated by story development.

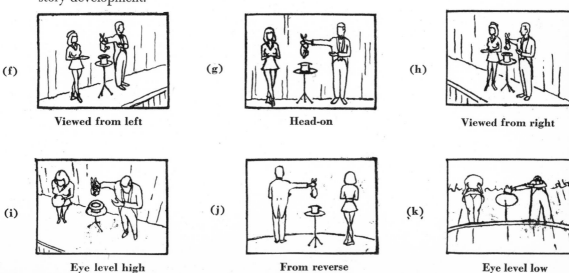

(f)   **(g)**   **(h)**

Viewed from left   **Head-on**   **Viewed from right**

(i)   **(j)**   **(k)**

Eye level high   **From reverse**   **Eye level low**

7. LINE . . .

LINE describes the predominant design of the picture composition. Line exerts a psychological effect upon a spectator as well as facilitating emphasis in the picture. The use of line can aid or hinder the psychological development of the story. Its use should always be motivated toward a specific end. Line is what the eye remembers.

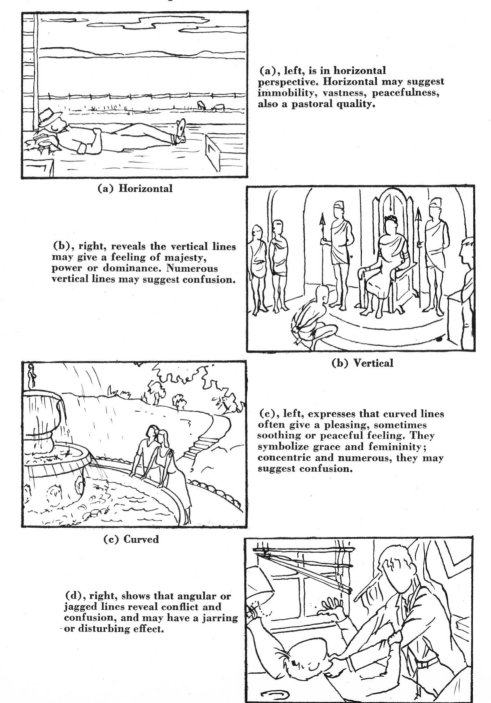

(a), left, is in horizontal perspective. Horizontal may suggest immobility, vastness, peacefulness, also a pastoral quality.

(a) Horizontal

(b), right, reveals the vertical lines may give a feeling of majesty, power or dominance. Numerous vertical lines may suggest confusion.

(b) Vertical

(c), left, expresses that curved lines often give a pleasing, sometimes soothing or peaceful feeling. They symbolize grace and femininity; concentric and numerous, they may suggest confusion.

(c) Curved

(d), right, shows that angular or jagged lines reveal conflict and confusion, and may have a jarring or disturbing effect.

(d) Angular

SUGGESTED WORKING DEMONSTRATIONS

For Individual and Group Evaluation
"If the theory is wrong, the practice cannot be right."

1. Using a window and door as a background, arrange several pieces of furniture for visual form and motivational values.

2. Stage the action for the following:

(a) A Boy's Club meeting.

(b) Distinguished Men's Club meeting.

(c) Three characters, each one believing the others crazy.

(1) One supporting an issue.
(2) Others suppressing an issue.

(d) An individual or a group of stockholders waiting for a decision of the Board of Directors of a large corporation.

(e) A confession.

(f) A parent ordering son or daughter from his or her house.

(g) A son introducing his bride to his family. The family sees the girl for the first time and rejects her because of her race.

Chapter 6

AUDIBLE ELEMENTS

...Selection of Dramatic
Audio Components...
...The Appropiate Expression
of Effect...
When You See...When You Hear
...Visual Complement...

SELECTION OF DRAMATIC AUDIO COMPONENTS

THE SOUND TRACK . . .

Sound can be used to emphasize, distort, reflect, distract, combine, and direct the physical and emotional attention to an action in the drama.

The picture dictates the sound. Sound on film can be formed into artistic material as motion can be captured on a still photo.

CINEMATIC STRUCTURE . . .

Cinematic structure is not built solely by the camera, but rather by a combination of the many channels of cinematic techniques. Sound is one of those channels. The sound track with the picture completes the story for the audience.

The components of sound are:

DIALOGUE. The dialogue projects theme, plot and character.

BACKGROUND EFFECTS. Background effects aid in projecting atmosphere and environment.

MUSIC AND MUSIC EFFECTS. Music underscores scenes, thus helping to render an emotional spirit to what is seen or what is about to be seen.

SOUND. As a Consideration to Story . . .

Sound *creates* a consciousness for the mood of the story. It promotes the ability to feel emotion.

Sound *motivates* the story and expresses details of the environment, mood, atmosphere and spirit.

Sound *intensifies* the action.

Sound *has continuity* and advances the emotional elements, especially the elements dealing with theme.

Sound *has character* and creates expectancy of corresponding visual elements.

Sound is dramatic in floods, fires, explosions, wars, wrecks, catastrophies and other such situations. The effect of sound may lie also in its relative absence.

What the ear hears and interprets as silence is not, in most cases, complete absence of sound, but rather absence of what the ear interprets as noise, i.e., the silence of the innermost chamber of a cave deep in the earth is different from the silence of a beautiful meadow, a forest or a prairie.

THE APPROPRIATE EXPRESSION OF EFFECT

Sound effects sharpen an experience and cause the drama to heighten as it unfolds. The discovery and matching of "life-like" sound to pictures require foresight and preparation.

Underwater, the action of a skin diver is heightened by the sounds of the bubbles combined with eerie music, as he moves cautiously through the murky water.

When accompanying an establishing shot, such as the one on the right, the sound of the angry surf throwing itself upon the beach presents an ominous atmosphere which prepares the audience for scenes to come . . .

Sound effects give a picture more meaning. The achievement of the proper effect, by sound, is a challenge to the imagination. In order for these effects to have their greatest value, they must be so constructed that the audience is not aware of them, per se.

AUDITORY INTERPRETATION . . .

The tendency of the beginner and occasionally of the professional in films and television production is to forget the importance and dramatic effect of sound. It must be remembered that sound complements the visual, and a competent director will never overlook its usefulness.

Sound should be regarded with as much respect as the composition of the picture. Life is found in complete correspondence between what the eye sees and what the ear hears.

All sound has perspective which is varied through pitch, volume and quality. By pitch, volume and quality we can tell from which direction a sound comes—from far or near, a cellar, a large hall, a small room, or out-of-doors.

Through pitch and quality of voice, we can identify a character as young, old, male or female. By the same method, we can also identify the character's various emotional states.

The use of sound can create emotional reaction in an audience. Sound completes the illusion of what the viewer sees. Sound must, therefore, be as carefully composed as any other factor of the story.

PERSPECTIVE IN SOUND . . .

Sound has the same character in one part of space as another; it can only be louder or softer, closer or more distant. It can be mixed with other sounds in different ways, such as with music, chatter, and noises. The relationship of sound to atmosphere must be governed by the balance and distance in the actual picture created in the production.

Sound forms atmosphere behind the speech of an actor. Sound in the background assists an audience in associating an emotional attitude with the idea of a scene.

THE DIRECTOR AND SOUND . . .

Sound helps the director tell the story. The absence of sound leaves the visual elements in a composition only partially completed, thus reducing the power of their emotional values.

The director must learn how to communicate with sound as well as with the picture. He must carefully research the story in order to properly fit sound with both the character and environment.

THE AUDIENCE AND SOUND . . .

The proper use of sound creates an emotional quality in a scene. In order to express the emotion realistically, sound should give insight to the picture and create meaningful experience for the audience.

Sound completes the action and focuses the attention of the audience. It outlines and enhances the emphasis of the composition, thus creating awareness of the dramatic moment in the mood intended.

To deal with sound realistically for the cinematic media, requires a visual and audible correspondence. The microphone and the camera combine to explore the world of reality. They transmit people in conversation and the sounds of their environment.

WHEN YOU SEE—WHEN YOU HEAR—An Illusion is Completed

Sound is a Visual Complement

Sound completes the illusion of reality. It must have perspective combined with the character of the composition. It fulfills the spirit of a scene.

Sound plays suspense. For example: In the motion picture, "Thirty Seconds Over Tokyo", directed by Mervyn Leroy, there is a scene inside a plane in which the men in the bomber are on their way to bomb Tokyo. Director Leroy used a steady drone of the airplane motor to create suspense. The sound was kept on the sound track for a reel and a half. By the time the target was sighted, the suspense was terrific.

The nature of sound is discovered in the character of a scene—a door creaking, a window closing, footsteps, etc. It has the ability to carry an overtone of excitement and sensation.

SILENCE AND THE PICTURE . . .

Silence in the film media is not the absence of sound. Silence has character. The silence of a tunnel is identifiably different from the silence of a deserted city street. If from the top of a high place, or from somewhere far, we can distinguish a sound we can identify—if we can hear the night sound of an animal—the flap of wings—the buzz of a mosquito as it fills the room—the distant wail of a train— then we are aware of the silence around us.

"NOISE" EXTERNAL SOUND . . .

Noise is a complex of sound—a mixture. It can be comparable to white light, which consists of a mixture of light of all different colors.

Rain . . . a drop or . . .

DIALOGUE AND SOUND . . .

The form of sound, combined with the dialogue, is a dramatic design of contrast. Dialogue is oral communication between people, which serves as an extension or supplement to pantomime in expressing ideas.

Dialogue may be a series of words or it may be one word. As one picture may contain the meaning of many words, so can one word extend its force or impact. Dramatic dialogue is richly suggestive. It is full of imagery.

The dialogue can be made to fulfill the function of sound in the drama. As in real life, it serves to broaden the scope of action.

At times, the dialogue may be conceived with imagination, and yet be void of effect. The words of exchange and impelling drives create and make possible the contrast needed for the audience to feel the impact and drama of the story.

SOUND AND EFFECT—VISUAL COMPLEMENT . . .

Sound must appear to arise from the action. Sound acts as a part of the emotional "nerve center" of the dramatic pattern. Sound has a language of its own, the speech of things and words.

VISUAL COMPLEMENT

The effects of sound, with the picture and without dialogue, can be significant and very dramatic.

. . . The pregnant silence

The incessant ringing of . . .

. . . The thundering . . .

A SOUND . . . then the verdict is . . .

THE PLOT: "With Intent to Kill!"

. . . Silence?

STORY: . . . WITH INTENT TO KILL!

"SCENE ONE"—"TAKE ONE"—"SOUND ONE"

(The Master Shot)

"SCENE TWO"—"TAKE TWO"—"SOUND TWO"

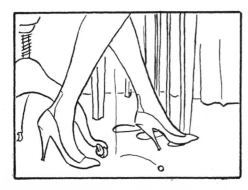

. . . a crashing **SOUND** from the piano . . .

. . . a single bead dropping, then . . .

"SCENE THREE"—"TAKE THREE"—"SOUND THREE"

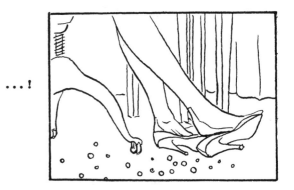

...!

SYNCHRONIZATION . . .

The total realization affecting the presentation of the drama requires the harmonic arrangement of all audible effects with the action of the picture.

The dramatic composition in the motion picture is a synthesis of the elements of the drama. It is designed to impress and control the emotions of an audience.

The unities of a dramatic presentation mean the unities of time, place and action, also the unities of sound, picture and the technical arts which affect the product of the drama.

Synchronization, therefore, is the total effect of sound and picture.

RECORDING . . .

The mechanical means for capturing various sound elements on tape or film is referred to as the recording step or process.

These are:

(1) DIALOGUE. Speech, narration.

(2) SOUND EFFECTS—Such as the noise of a car, a door closing on stage and off, the drop of a spoon, the shot of a gun—etc.

(3) MUSIC—Either original or from a music library including records, film or tape.

(4) ATMOSPHERE—The perspective mood of a place for the editor.

RE-RECORDING . . .

The mechanical means of combining the above separate sound elements onto one sound track, is the process of re-recording.

This process serves to reproduce the combined total effect of all tracks into a final product.

The total sound track is then synchronized with the picture elements which, in turn, are projected to the audience.

TOTAL EFFECT . . .

The sound track is as important as the picture to the total impression on the audience. Therefore, care must be exercised in the selection of the audible elements which complement the story, and also in the technical excellence of the recording of the master sound track—especially in the synchronization process.

If the sound is not synchronized technically, as well as in its selection, the effect can destroy the impact of a total production.

Chapter 7

BLENDING AUDIO-VISUAL ELEMENTS

...Technique of Editing Film
...The Film Editor...Story
and Creative Intention...
...Selection...Pictorial
Pattern...

THE FILM MEDIUM

The recorded history of the audio-visual media is a series of scientific advances leading to the development of modern film technology. It is a series of artistic and dramatic developments culminating in present-day film production techniques.

In the film media, as in the legitimate theatre, the physical preparation of the story is done outside the playing area. The proscenium is only a frame which embodies that portion of the production seen by the audience. The extension of the psychological field of performance and the freedom of a plane of time allows the story to be projected beyond the confines of the playing areas found on the legitimate stage.

The film medium is a method by which changing emotions can be projected through a series of visual changes. This technique of visual changes allows the audience to accept the characterizations and respond emotionally to the story elements. The film a most effective story telling medium. It is flexible in visual and audible perspectives.

The film creates an illusion of reality—a "you are there" quality and feeling in terms of setting and environment that is unique.

Because the camera can "take in" many details or can emphasize a single detail of a scene, the film originator and interpreter can control, direct and develop the audience response in a pre-determined way through selection of visual images. The audible elements of the image must complement this selection.

The pattern of life-like sounds and effects extends and accelerates the reality of the visual image. It offers a tempo of rhythmic expression for the movements of the action, thus increasing the flow of theatrical expressiveness for the audience. Such patterns of expression are the result of many editing processes undertaken in producing a film production.

BLENDING AUDIO-VISUAL ELEMENTS INTO STORY

Human development is in reality gradual and often takes place over a long period of time. The film media exist on a timeless plane. They can capsulate a long period of development into an actual short period of time by selecting the visual and audible essence of the development which is arranged with continuity and transition.

The end product is realistic in the sense of the essentials of the development, but representational in that it omits unimportant details or speeds up the realistic long period of time of the actual development.

A film may show the unfolding of a tight bud into a full-blown blossom in less than a minute, yet the actual blossoming may have taken several days. A lifetime may span seventy-five years, but a film may represent the essence of that life in two hours or less. Generations may span hundreds of years, but a film may relate the essence of such a history in less than two hours.

When a director has analyzed a story and has covered with film footage the scope of his interpretation, the film editor then, through arrangement of the parts of the film footage, completes the expression for its fullest audience impact. In cinematic technique and in the art of expression, the story content is always a process of pursuit of ideas and stimulation.

The film editor's job begins when the director finishes his "shooting". The film editor then blends the audio-visual elements into a fluid story.

CREATIVE INTENTION

THE FILM EDITOR—The Principles of Scripting, Directing, Effects, Photography, Music and Sound Composition Bound Together.

The film editor is a creative artist. He is known as the film architect —one who assembles the pictures, sound tracks, music and music effects, picture and picture effects into a narrative fabric that will unfold on the screen in the most dramatic and entertaining way possible.

STORY AND CREATIVE INTENTION

The film editor must consider the creative intention of the film's originators. He must clearly understand the story—the writer's concept, the producer's aims, the director's intent and the audience for whom the film is intended.

Editing film is a psychological and physical process of selection. Its effectiveness rests in its sudden and bold surprises, its exciting and logical changes, and movements from one specific visualization to another. The editor controls the story through the juxtaposition of the visual, audible and emotional elements of each scene.

SELECTION—Pictorial Pattern

The key to the editor's success and, consequently, to the production's success is the editor's analysis, judgment and selection of the film. It must be skillfully blended to achieve the effect which will fulfill the originator's creative intention.

No rules or standards for this film blending can be stated as infallible, since each story has a different tale to tell. Editing is objective creativity rather than a personal point of view. In the editor's work, the film itself evolves as the principal "personality."

The film editor depends upon the director's coverage of the story. The director depends upon the editor's selection of the scenes, which controls the pace of the story. The editor, in deciding a pictorial pattern, must consider where the action came from, where it is, and where it will go next.

THE EDITOR'S FUNCTION . . .

The director orders the scenes to be photographed from a variety of angles, thus providing the editor with the possibility of choice in constructing a finished sequence.

The film editor cannot creatively develop a film story without enough footage to give him a choice of cut-in and cut-away scenes which fit the sequence with which he is working.

Therefore, the director covers each master scene of a story he shoots with differing points of view.

The exposed footage may be equal to a ratio of two, three, four, five or more times the footage of the completed film. The director determines the ratio based upon: (1) the possible combinations of points of view that an editor may use in developing the film story, and (2) the provision of differing points of view for relief of any visually static scenes, and (3) the provision of footage to cover sufficient orientation expansion, compression or emotional control of the visual composition and (4) any errors or changes in visual and sound composition.

After the final cut by the editor, there may be miles of footage which will be discarded or indexed for future use. Of this discarded footage, portions may be taken for stock library use. These portions so used are referred to as "out-takes".

It seems that the editor is in full creative charge after the completion of principal photography. However, after each "completed" cut, both director and producer view the editor's work before the final cut is made and the end product is reached through the combined efforts of all three.

The director's responsibility is to capture the images on film. The editor is primarily responsible for constructing this raw material into a completed product.

The editor's judgment in film selection and continuity is a guide to heightening the effectiveness of the total story for the viewer. Each piece of film must be judged for acting performance, artistic camera work, story continuity of action, coverage and transitional elements.

It is a long process of adding and subtracting, over-dramatizing and under-dramatizing, juggling and making transitions till the best arrangement of material for expressing the story is discovered. The editor must be concerned with proper timing of scenes and dialogue so as to pace the film for its dramatic content.

The editor must be concerned with and use his judgment of continuity and transition to blend the audible elements of sound to the visualization. He must bring to bear any or all techniques to achieve a total effect, which will involve the audience in the story without making the audience aware of the techniques. In short, he must blend the audio-visual elements for the best total effect—a finished product. This calls for disciplined patience and skill as well as imagination and daring.

Chapter 8

INTERPRETING THE SCENARIO

...The Scenario: Translation
of Story into Film Story...
Systematic Process by Which
Action is Evaluated...
A Plan for Story Action...

THE SCENARIO—Translation of Story into Film Story

Film structure unfolds through gradual changes, development, and advancement. The arrangement of these elements must be so constructed that they clearly define contrasts in character and story. A scenario, therefore, is a set of plans which points out the course of action. It is a plan of action.

The writer must have his source of materials under control so the form and order of story development may advance logically with meaning and purpose. The entire pattern of the story should be carefully analyzed for significant motivation.

The story is written in scenario structure, with marked sequential divisions expressing continuous action making it possible for the interpreters to reproduce the flow of life-like experiences.

We must assume that the story has already been written, at least in treatment form, by the scenarist or someone else.

The scenarist's job is to tell the story in sound and visual images. The scenario contains not only dialogue but directions for creating sound and pictures. These directions may include directions for camera movement, stage business, setting, lighting, make-up, sound perspective, effects and music.

SOUND AND VISUAL IMAGES

The writer must "think" with his eyes and ears, as well as with his mind, in order to project the ideas of a story to an audience. The writer must develop his material in terms of theme, environment, character, plot and situation so that their interrelated artistic values can be expressed in the production by the director, actor and technician.

A good scenario is as indispensible to the originators and interpreters of a film production as a set of plans to an architect. Writing directly for film is a technique which requires imagination in the use of the elements of a picture and sound composition.

The director must be given specific information regarding the development of the character and the theme. The plot lives by the strategy and the quick, startling changes that appear in a composition of experience—the difference between telling a story and dramatizing one. Every given moment expressed by a thought, either appearing in the dialogue or covered in the action or emphasized through a reaction, must be analyzed and motivated. Otherwise believability is lost.

A good scenario, when properly translated, creates the rhythm and "beats" of a story. The scenario provides the director, technician, artist and management with a basic delineation by which the production may be prepared before being exposed to the camera and microphone. By doing this, the producer, director and the technicians determine length, budget, props, settings, locations, lights, sundry equipment, cast and materials to organize and formulate a production pattern which helps solve many production problems.

The story material for novel, stage, screen and radio/television demands form. The form itself plays a decisive and determining role both in a production and how the production will appear to the audience. The final form of a scenario determines how a producer must work, how a director will work, how the artist should work and what the audience will finally see.

Many directors write their own scenarios—and for a good reason. They write in full recognition and control of their own resources and limitations for the production.

The director-writer can easily develop characterizations which are related to his directional style. He can further develop the plot and many other aspects of the production. He can space sequences for timing and pacing as he films and records sound. He may develop more of a dimension for the story. He may direct the camera's eye more understandingly to express his interpretation of the story, by writing a plan of action which will enable him as a director to translate story into living performance.

Whether or not a director writes his own scenario, it is extremely important to his success that he thoroughly understand the interpretation of the story.

The terminology and format of a scenario forms a "universal language" for all originators and interpreters concerned with film production.

CREATIVE INTENTION

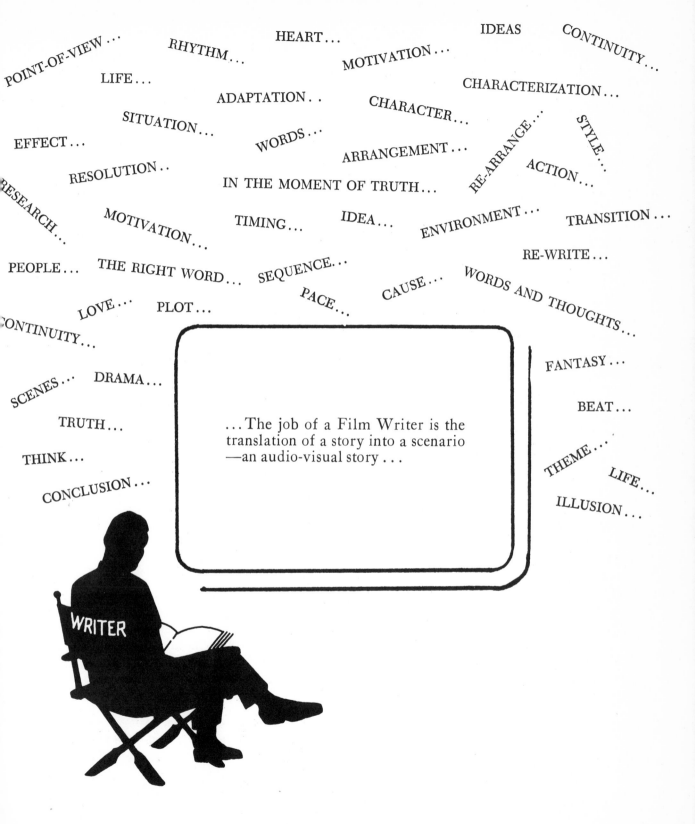

POINT-OF-VIEW... RHYTHM... HEART... IDEAS CONTINUITY...

LIFE... MOTIVATION... CHARACTERIZATION...

ADAPTATION.. CHARACTER...

SITUATION... WORDS... RE-ARRANGE... STYLE...

EFFECT... ARRANGEMENT... ACTION...

RESOLUTION.. IN THE MOMENT OF TRUTH... RE-ARRANGE...

RESEARCH... MOTIVATION... TIMING... IDEA... ENVIRONMENT... TRANSITION...

PEOPLE... THE RIGHT WORD... SEQUENCE... RE-WRITE...

LOVE... PLOT... PACE... CAUSE... WORDS AND THOUGHTS...

CONTINUITY...

SCENES... DRAMA... FANTASY...

BEAT...

TRUTH... ...The job of a Film Writer is the translation of a story into a scenario —an audio-visual story...

THINK... THEME...

LIFE...

CONCLUSION... ILLUSION...

WRITER

SYSTEMATIC PROCESS BY WHICH ACTION IS EVALUATED

A story forms itself in the mind's-eye of the author and is an expression of his thoughts. Every story must have a beginning, a middle and an end.

The story may be presented first as a PREMISE, second as a TREATMENT and finally in its elaborated form, the ADAPTATION which is the scenario or screenplay.

<u>*S T O R Y*</u>

(a)	(b)	(c)
A Springboard	A Development	A Resolution
PREMISE	TREATMENT	ADAPTATION

(a) The SPRINGBOARD presents the basic conflict between the principal characters or situation and idea in the story. It is that portion of the plot which captures the attention of the audience.

(b) The DEVELOPMENT shows the events as they occur, the changes that take place and where the basic conflict of the characters is brought to a climax.

(c) The RESOLUTION is the ending. This may be either a logical or natural ending, depending upon the characters, the plot, the theme, the subject or the idea.

PREMISE

A Premise is short, terse, the explanation of the story told simply as possible. A premise can usually be explained in one or two sentences.

TREATMENT

The Treatment is a complete preparation of the story prior to writing the final scenario. The treatment entails a development of the basic situation, the plot and the characters in detailed description. The object of a treatment is to conjure for the reader what the full action of the story is as it takes place. In the writing of the treatment, only key dialogue need be included.

ADAPTATION

The elaboration of premise and/or treatment constitutes the scenario or adaptation.

THE SCENE—A UNIT OF ACTION

The scene is identified with the time, place and function. The scene, when organized, defines the atmosphere, setting and characters involved in an event. It is a division of a story, which is part of a sequence. It is a unit of action in a given environment and is placed in sequential form and order.

The scene expresses the essential thoughts required for complete understanding of the action. Every action is the inevitable result of the preceding actions. The scene can be fixed at a given angle or motivated as a whole action in the situation, thus completing a defined movement.

All scenes must be numbered for identification. The numbers, starting with "one" and progressing in sequential order, must appear beside each scene.

Identification of every scene is important to the laboratory processing, handling and editing. The number of a scene is the main point of reference for anyone who uses the scenario and is as important as the title of the story.

The scene in sequence is not only the method by which the action is organized to motivate a dramatic result, but the rearrangement in which the mechanics advance the pictorial essence in continuity.

The break between one scene and the next leads to the remedy and reason, the meaning and actual effect of the action. The result is in the climax and development of the action as it turns out. The action in scenes must be broken up, as they advance, between what is happening and the probability of the event.

The director who understands what motivates and provokes action, should be able to transform a scenario into a living story. The director must think in terms of motivation which produces the transitions of a story and defines time and characterization, which move the plot and theme of a story to a conclusion.

THE SITUATION—STORY MATERIAL

The situation grows out of the character and theme of the story. Every story begins with a situation that is reorganized and developed during the course of the action.

For example: A woman sits before a mirror wondering about her husband. She has tears in her eyes as she goes to the phone and calls.

The scene shifts to his office as the phone rings. The husband doesn't answer.

Shortly thereafter, the husband phones to say he'll be a little late coming home. We see him at that moment in a night club with another woman.

The scene shifts back to the wife. The audience knows the situation. The situation provides a source of motivation for action which expresses emotional or physical response. The situation may then be defined as the pattern of circumstances affecting behavior and determining character response.

THE ENVIRONMENT—EXPRESSIVE, DRAMATIC ATMOSPHERE

Generally, the first thing one does is to indicate the kind of environmental atmosphere in which he wishes his characters to move:

...Is the atmosphere light or heavy?

...Romantic or tragic?

...Located in country, town or a city?

   Is it a street, road, farm, desert, forest, seashore,
      air, water, mountain or the moon?

...Night or day? Dusk or dawn?

...Snowing or raining? Sunny or cloudy?

   Fog? Hot? Cold? etc.

Environment is a primary aid to creating mood. It is a definite part of any story. It can contribute or detract from the story, for everything seen by the camera becomes an integral part of the action.

Environment presents a perspective in BACKGROUND (b.g.) in scenario terminology where the principal action is played. The environment in a western provides a setting that is physically impressive— the expanse of mountain and prairie, horses and cattle, sounds and things as they actually exist in power and scope.

The environment in a poor home is different from that of a family of wealth.

The background should always be clearly defined—active or passive, vivid or dull, sharp or diffused. The action must be seen in the proper environmental atmosphere and it must be logically interpreted by the interpreter.

THEME—MAIN STORY INGREDIENT

A theme is the central idea of a story. It is the "heart" of the story— its main ingredient. A theme is woven into the elements of the story and should be discovered by the audience.

The theme can be discovered in the experiences and nature of the characters and in the relationship of these to the environment of the story. The theme is best described in terms of the universals of love, hate, fear, sex, greed, ambition, jealousy, etc.

CHARACTER—STORY PORTRAYAL

The action of a story may well be in the individual personality the actor portrays. A character defines specific personality, emotions and appearances peculiar to that person. The character develops with the plot but the plot arises from the characters.

Character and situation are necessary elements of the construction of each scene and sequence in the story. Characterization defines anything that differentiates one character in a story from another. Therefore, the character is an agent of the story.

PLOT—STORY MATERIAL

A plot lies in the invention, planning and strategy of exposing the action, and develops the actual material of a story. The characterizations are the key to the plot.

RESOLUTION—STORY'S TIME AND SIGNIFICANCE

A resolution in a story is found in the solution or ending of a dramatic problem.

Resolution may be considered as the controlling point of a dramatic movement, the saturation level, wherein the event or cycle of ideas is concluded, changed or solved.

Resolution ends, develops or creates a new balance of forces, conflicts and system of events.

Within the cycle of events there is the conclusion—the end of the action . . . "the moment of the last suspense."

A PLAN FOR STORY ACTION—Cinematic Technique

The following diagram is a plan for constructing a unit of action in a story. It is a step-by-step progression in cinematic story creation.

The writer constructs a single scene, which taken together with other scenes, is the foundation of cinematic story structure.

Beginning with a single SCENE (at the base of the triangle), the writer creates the elements of a scene with:

> (a) SITUATION
> (b) ENVIRONMENT
> (c) THEME
> (d) CHARACTER
> (e) PLOT
> (f) RESOLUTION

These elements of the scene must advance through TRANSITION from one element to the other. The transition may be effected by:

> (a) STORY Transition
> (b) CHARACTER Transition
> (c) MECHANICAL Transition

The scene must develop through appropriate:

> (a) ARRANGEMENT of its elements in—
> (b) CONTINUITY to establish the writer's—
> (c) POINT OF VIEW in a SEQUENCE

The development of the scene culminates (at the apex of the triangle) in a UNIT OF ACTION which is, within the frame of reference of the scene, logically caused and resultant from that cause. The UNIT OF ACTION is the SCENE.

The same plan which is followed in the construction of a single scene is also followed in the construction of a story composed of many scenes.

A PLAN FOR ACTION

FOUNDATION FOR STORY

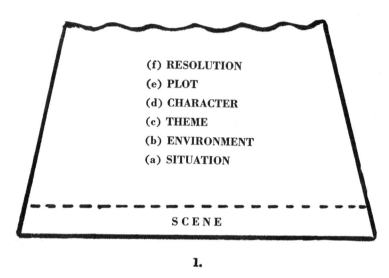

(f) RESOLUTION
(e) PLOT
(d) CHARACTER
(c) THEME
(b) ENVIRONMENT
(a) SITUATION

SCENE

1.

The scenes and sequences of the story form includes: SITUATION, ENVIRONMENT, THEME, CHARACTER, PLOT and RESOLUTION.

These are "ingredients" or elements from which scenes and sequences are constructed in parts that must be organized, much the same manner as the whole story.

The director must be able first to analyze a story and to interpret, from the adaptation, basic elements and then to project those elements through an artist to an audience.

The dramatization of a film story is composed of visual, audible, emotional and physical elements. The story begins when there is something to tell or react to and can be dramatized into a resolution.

A story for the audio-visual media is not intended to be read. The adaptation of a story into scenario must be interpreted so as to project the plot, theme, character, environment and situation through sound, dialogue and photographic movement. The atmospheric touches must focus attention and illustrate the essential elements.

The literary activity that goes into the creation of a film is a careful, creative process.

The scenario itself is the final result of such a process and becomes the FOUNDATION in a story projection.

TRANSITION—THE STORY PROGRESSION

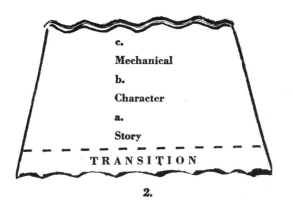

2.

Transition is a turning point in the story—a shift in the continuity. The entire complexion of a turning point in a story can change in one unit of action. It carries character, theme, environment, and plot from one development to another. Transition may be achieved by:

CHANGE, which may be effected MECHANICALLY—a DIS-SOLVE or a FADE, IN or OUT, designed for the audience.

STORY TRANSITION, which may be effected in the situation— the end of one sequence or the beginning of another.

CHARACTER TRANSITION, which may be effected by a complete change in the character with respect to his environment.

All film media are constructed of continuous transition. Transition in picture promotes the advancement of the story and moves photographic continuity in time and place. Transition in sound has continuity and carries the emotional element into basic resolution. The transition itself becomes an emotional and physical interpretation of the story as it resolves in a final conclusion. It separates changes in the development between sequences and compresses time, place and situation. It is a device for controlling the elements of the story.

SEQUENCE—SERIES OF ACTIONS

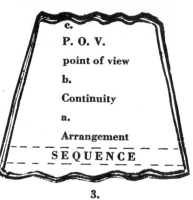

3.

A sequence is a division of a story made up of units, parts, scenes, shots, or "takes" which are formed in a sequential order. These scenes are thematically connected and related by order of occurrence. The sequences are then arranged in the order in which the sequential scenes are related in their continuity. The sequences of two or more scenes are prepared with a series of minor climaxes known as transitions. Sequences are arranged in continuity and in terms of length of action —the use of sound, dialogue and motivation. An entire sequence, made up of parts, is established as a division in a story. As scenes make up a sequence, so sequences make up a story. The events are arranged in continuity so that the geography of the whole story is established.

P.O.V. (POINT OF VIEW)—PERSPECTIVE OF ATTENTION

Point of view deals with the position from which an audience views each action in the story. Point of view is the perspective of attention so arranged that the emphasis will bring out reason and meaning. It is interpreted by the director in shaping the action for the audience.

ARRANGEMENT—PICTURE AND SOUND ORGANIZATION

Arrangement is the sequential organization of pictures and sound to define the director's interpretation for an audience. The director must be able to select his arrangement of action so that every emphasis and attention is easily and quickly related to the story elements as they advance.

The director must consider the mechanics in the arrangement of action in the pictorial content and sound continuity in each scene, where the action comes from, how it progresses and where it will go next. He must also consider its continuous movement in the very next frame of reference. As he changes the function of each scene, he must indicate where the character is at all times, his motivation—and the reason for change.

Change promotes variation and implies shifting circumstances, values or conditions that cause differences in the character of a scene with some regularity.

CONTINUITY—FORM OF STORY DEVELOPMENT

Continuity deals with the advancement of a series of actions, events, scenes, elements, dialogue and story values. It provides for the interconnecting of all actions.

Continuity deals with story structure, linkage and arrangement. It results from a plan for action.

Each unit of action projects a scene as it is established and allows it to move through an environment.

The director must be aware that the performance of a whole story for the audio-visual media is prepared from a deliberate order of action—When, Where, and How a story begins, develops and ends.

A UNIT OF ACTION—CAUSE, EFFECT

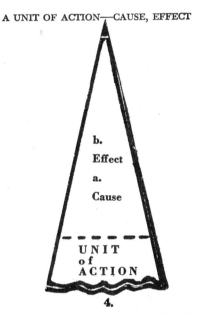

The cause of an action is the reaction to thought. A thought motivates an action. The resulting action may be physical behavior or an emotional response.

The significance of an action stresses effect and meaning. A change in action defines change to another point of view to which the mind in turn reacts. Motivation and change result from the need to emphasize and advance the story.

Reason and meaning determine the need for change. The result is a moving process of transition, which becomes an integral part of story structure.

A plan for action results in the construction of the SCENE which is the foundation of cinematic story structure.

When many scenes are put together with regard to—(a) SITUATION, (b) ENVIRONMENT, (c) THEME, (d) CHARACTER, (e) PLOT, (f) RESOLUTION, and are connected by effective TRANSITIONS in SEQUENCE, the result is a cinematic STORY.

Thus we see in the illustration, THE PLAN FOR STORY ACTION, that the same principles which adhere in the construction of the scene also adhere in the construction of the story composed of a number of scenes.

Interpreting the Scenario

A PLAN FOR STORY ACTION—

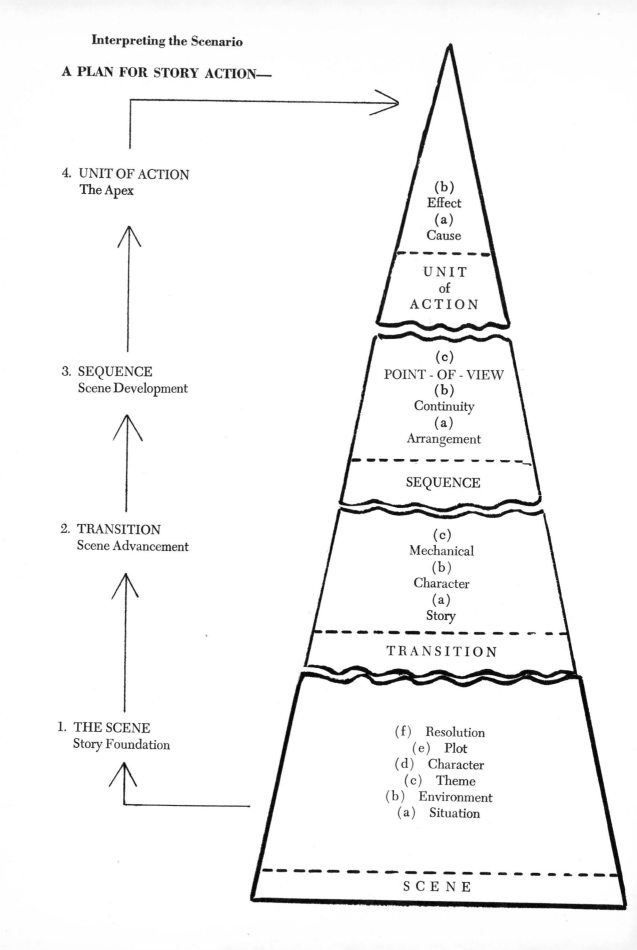

4. UNIT OF ACTION
   The Apex

3. SEQUENCE
   Scene Development

2. TRANSITION
   Scene Advancement

1. THE SCENE
   Story Foundation

(b) Effect
(a) Cause

UNIT
of
ACTION

(c) POINT - OF - VIEW
(b) Continuity
(a) Arrangement

SEQUENCE

(c) Mechanical
(b) Character
(a) Story

TRANSITION

(f) Resolution
(e) Plot
(d) Character
(c) Theme
(b) Environment
(a) Situation

SCENE

Chapter 9

SYSTEMATIC EVALUATION

Systematic Process for
Story Adaptation...
"Ingredients" of the Scenario
...The "Plotting" of the
Cinematic Form...Examples
of Photographic Form...
Self Assignment...

A screenplay presents characteristic, dramatic ingredients in motion as they appear in life. Writing is objectified thinking, whether it is one line, one page, or five hundred pages. The writer lives by his intention, ability, need to create. Writing is the externalized reality of the writer's imagination.

Writing for an audience involves the creation of ideas that molds words and action which will communicate. To the film writer, a story must always be interpreted into form that provides the realization of an experience which an audience will remember and recognize.

A story need not be realistic, but the story should stretch—be credible within its own frame of reference.

The audience likes interesting, human characters who fail as well as succeed. All of which boils down to one essential consideration. The writer must keep the audience constantly in mind as he creates a story.

The film writer must have an inherent knowledge of a director's working concept—the manner by which he interprets. He must be aware of the cinematic taste and judgment of the director of photography. He must understand the technical abilities of the team of artists and interpreters who create the images from the expression of his writing. He should be aware of the function of the film editor and the manner in which he completes the script's intent.

Writing is a fulfilment of ideas adapted into a dramatic form and translated by the various artists into believability.

The writer is an artist of individuality and his art is a form of rebellion. He rebels against the choking barriers of stereotyped form and, at times, against the conventional substance of ordinary living. He sees new forms of expression and strives to find an emotional release in keeping with his own individual discovery.

Writing can propose a philosophy, expound a religion and inspire creativity in others.

Film writing is a part of a universal language which is recognizable by the world audience. Yet, film writing, like all writing, is a lonely profession. The writer is always alone with his thoughts.

Exposition—A Capacity to
Develop Action

The writer who adapts a novel must consider how he will visualize the exposition as applied to action, situation, realization, cause and effect.

Exposition covers the possibilities and attitude of the drama. New detailed information is progressively presented. New conflicts and contrasts are added in the course and development of the drama. There are progressive changes in both character and environment.

The exposition is an action—the preparatory movement to a cycle of events which has its inner unity and defined limits. It exhibits the characteristic form of an action and climax. The exposition may also be divided into subordinate actions which develop to subordinate climaxes. Detailed exposition suggests to the creative interpreters how the director may stage the drama.

Dialogue—A Capacity for
Feeling

Dialogue is the chief vehicle for motivation and conveyance of necessary information in the development of situation. The writing of natural-sounding dialogue requires that a writer listen carefully to catch the essence of expressions people use.

Speech varies as much as appearance and personality. Natural speech changes just as much as the facial expressions of the characters speaking the lines. A good writer can use speech to reveal his characters.

Words in dialogue present a tempo and a pace of their own. There is an inherent rhythm in the sound of a word. The visualization of the character who listens and reacts to the meaning is just as important as the character who speaks his thoughts.

There is a subtle relationship between dialogue and camera movement. However, words alone can carry the momentum of the scene without camera movement.

Some directors use a technique which starts an extended dialogue passage with the camera some distance away from the principals, then slowly, almost imperceptibly moving in, building to a subtle climax.

Another technique is that in which the camera cuts away and scans the movement of the characters, or the camera cuts away on other subjects while the dialogue is spoken.

Dialogue promotes the movement of the characters or the camera, making the drama significantly pleasurable to see, hear and react to.

The Story Treatment

Dialogue used in a treatment is called the key dialogue. In a treatment, only that dialogue is included which will be dramatically effective. Otherwise, what is being said should be described.

For example: Jane becomes very angry at Joe and tells him she will leave him.

The descriptive line: . . ."tells him she will leave him." is a dramatic speech and should be expressed in dialogue in this manner: . . . Jane is furious, she turns to Joe, her eyes blazing, she screams, "I'm leaving you!"

The length of a treatment can be anywhere from three to three-hundred pages. One of the purposes of the treatment may be to sell the story before a completely detailed shooting scenario is written. Every producing company has unique production policies and very often its requirements for the actual scenario will differ.

Another purpose of the treatment is to crystalize the story line. Free-lance writers often write both treatment and scenario before sale.

Finally, the treatment serves to structure the scenario. A treatment is to a writer what a sales talk is to a salesman. The treatment, then, is a detailed, extremely selective story told in terms of cinematic technique.

The writing of a scenario begins with a treatment. The next step is the blocked outline from which the scenes are written for the screenplay.

1. Example: Step-One—
"The Story Treatment"

Mrs. Jane Doe is in the kitchen of her small apartment, washing the supper dishes. Her husband, Joe, absent for several nights, enters. He has obviously been drinking. She reprimands him severely and threatens to leave him. Going into the bedroom, she begins throwing her clothes into a suitcase. Joe goes into the living room and takes a gun out of the desk drawer. He then follows Jane into the bedroom.

"You're never gonna leave me!" Joe fires once, then twice, then again, and Jane slumps to the floor. The distraught man gasps as he looks at the limp body. He drops the gun and moves to the telephone and dials the operator.

2. Example: Step-Two—
"Blocked Outline"

1. JANE DOE is washing the dishes. Her husband, JOE, enters the room. They argue. Jane says she is going to leave him. She exits.

2. We find Jane in her bedroom as she gets her suitcase and begins throwing clothes into it.

3. Back in the living room, Joe goes to his desk and gets a gun from the drawer.

4. In the bedroom, Joe enters with the gun, tells Jane she'll never leave him, then shoots her.

5. Joe, shocked at what he has done, drops the gun, goes into the living room, picks up the phone and dials.

Notice that the scenes in the blocked outline are now numbered and identified as to where the action is located. Characters are in CAPS the first time they are introduced. The description of the action and dialogue in the scene is single spaced.

When the BLOCKED OUTLINE is completed, the writer should have everything he needs on paper to write the scenario. Next comes the actual dialogue and the individual camera angles and shots.

A Story Idea, for example . . .

Jane went to the mirror, sat down on
the chair and looked at her face.

The TREATMENT of this same story idea written in the present tense is told as it is happening.

Jane goes to the mirror, sits down on
the chair and looks at her face.

A BLOCKED OUTLINE is written solely for the writer's own edification and use. The outline is used as a guide.

To construct the outline, refer to the TREATMENT and set it down in short, terse paragraphs, numbering them consecutively from "one" to as many scenes as the screenplay requires. Establish the location of the scene and describe the situation in terms of action.

The adaptation is referred to as a scenario or a shooting script. Its physical appearance, terminology, arrangement and marked divisions are specific and in character with film structure. Since the film story is told by the camera and microphone, the composition of the photographic images must be arranged in succession, as a story, and include all dialogue, visual and audible effects. The screenplay indicates to the director, art directors, cameramen, actors and craftsmen, the actual types of scenes and script requirements. Too much detail is confusing; too little detail may not sufficiently inform the interpreters and the craftsmen as to what is necessary to convey the story mood.

From the screenplay, the production supervisor makes a "breakdown" in terms of time, rehearsals, materials, construction and costs. The production supervisor must indicate to the entire production staff the following:

Sets and scenes; scheduling, day and date; scenes and sequences; night and day; picture and sound; special effects; props and vehicles; special props; special equipment; cast (speaking and non-speaking); extras and others in background; detail of atmosphere; special make-up and wardrobe; and all locations and pertinent information relating to production.

The classifications of items for a "breakdown" will generally be the same, but the form will depend upon the policies of the producing organization. Everything concerned with the entire production must be detailed on paper. This is what is meant by "breakdown".

"INGREDIENTS" OF THE SCENARIO

THE MASTER SCENE—In principle this scene is obligatory and establishes orientation. It tells where you are, night or day, inside or outside, what the situation is about and the people involved.

THE EXPOSITION—The exposition is an action in changes-contrasts-conflicts. It covers the possibilities of a scene, connecting the action with a theme. It is the means of plotting the framework of a story. It is the working description of staging and it sets forth the content of a scene.

The exposition introduces the characters and their relationships and attitudes towards each other. It is physically placed before dialogue.

The exposition conveys the story mood, the environment and the atmosphere to all those concerned with the script. This type of exposition is not to be confused with dialogue exposition.

DIALOGUE EXPOSITION—At certain points in the story, the writer finds he must explain or convey specific information to the audience which expresses a reason for a situation in which the characters find themselves. For example:

JANE:

... We've lived in this apartment
for five years now ... and all the
time you've been floating from
job to job and ...

The author has planted, with this short expository dialogue, that Jane and her husband have been arguing the fact that he has not settled down to a steady job. It also indicates there is something else between them. It establishes the relationship between the two.

THE DIALOGUE—The expressions which plot and move the action constitutes "dialogue." It is full of expressed and communicated ideas. From the dialogue comes motivation.

THE CONTINUITY—Continuity deals with the advancement of the actions and story. The scenario defines the scene-by-scene action and the various compositional elements in fluid continuity.

In live television, continuity is in sequence as the play progresses on the set. The single units of action are automatically linked as in a play on the stage.

In motion pictures, the continuity must be contained in the script, because the actual shooting is in single units, and will not necessarily follow the sequence and the continuity of the story. Economy and efficiency dictate filming all scenes of a script which utilize the same location.

Availability of cast, crew, equipment, rigging, lighting units for the specific location and setting often dictate the order in which units of action are filmed. The joining together in continuity comes later in the editing room.

THE TRANSITION—The transition allows for contrasts from one part of the story developing into the next phase dealing with time, theme, place, plot and character. Transition deals with the foreshadowing and conclusions of dramatic actions.

THE SOUND TRACK—The sound track brings the story to life. The sound track is a process of synchronization involving dialogue, effects, music and atmosphere. Sound intensifies the senses of the audience. For example:

The scene is a small home near the sea. A sailor, saying goodbye to his wife, is seen, while in sound, the *creak* of a baby rocker is blended with the sound of the *pounding* surf.

Sound effects drive the action. Sound has the character of reaction. Sound helps the story unfold with the dialogue. Sound carries the emotional load of the story into a basic resolution.

For example, quoted from a screenplay of "THE CHOSEN" by Arthur Ripley:

> . . . ."When the dissolve clears, the morning sun has replaced the monstrance. A meadowlark calls in the distance. Far off is heard the mournful wail of the commuter train. OVER THE SCENE from the inside of the building again is heard the piercing clang of one of the corridor bells."

Note the following examples (from the same screenplay) of the total effect of sound:

> . . ."THE CAMERA PANS AWAY from the priests as the piercing sound of the bell is sustained through the DISSOLVE, and blends with the sound of an approaching siren as the DISSOLVE CLEARS.
>
> The sound of horns, the music coming from a hurdy-gurdy, and voices are heard as we open on a CLOSEUP of a shining policeman's badge.
>
> THE CAMERA PULLS AWAY disclosing a crowd of people gathered around a tall figure dressed in a long black robe, his body sprawled around a bicycle lying on the street". . .

Sound is not only expressed in a screenplay but can also be expressed in a treatment:

> This is a tenement section in a large city. The area is near a *railroad.* It is mid-July. The time is day, *children are chattering, laughing* and running in and out of *water pouring* out of a fire hydrant.
> *Trucks and automobiles* make their way slowly through the busy, narrow street. Inside a tenement flat, the sound of a baby's *cry* is heard. We find a woman entering from another room in the house. She holds a small baby bottle in her hands as she moves to the window. The *shrill whistle* of a train mixed with the *clatter of wheels* becomes louder and louder.
> *Noises of traffic,* the *chatter of children* on the street below, added to the *water splashing,* fills the room. The woman closes the window and the outside noises fade in the background. Now the *baby's cry* is heard and we can hear the *music* coming from a small radio. The woman turns the dial and the music stops.

The effect of life, in the organization of the picture, is derived from the sounds which a director is able to select from, in and around the environment where the character lives.

The effect derived from the sounds of life is a natural development in the organization of a story. The story becomes significantly illuminated to the audience when the sound, music, and natural effects are synchronized with the visual action.

The framework of imagination lies in the use of sound effects. The immediate response to the realities draws the audience into the action.

The director will discover that to experience the sound, in effect, is compatible to the impression created by the character for the audience.

SOUND AND PICTURE—The synchronization of the sound with picture is the completion of a screenplay pattern from which the director, artist, and technician can translate ideas, story, plot, character, theme and situation into composite composition. Such synchronization is a creative process as it unfolds the elements of environment, emotion and characterization in their relationships for and to an audience.

THE "PLOTTING" OF THE CINEMATIC FORM

The scenario is an accepted form in which a story is prepared for motion picture production.

The staging and general description of the scene always appears, in form, before the dialogue. It tells something of the scene, indicates the motivated action and introduces the characters.

The general description of the action must be written so that it suggests the working cues to the director, from which he derives a mood or an attitude.

Scripts usually start with FADE IN and end with FADE OUT. Two or more blank spaces down from the first direction of "FADE-IN", we have the camera direction in CAPS. At the beginning of any sequence, or the introduction of change in the physical setting, we must indicate certain general points.

The identification of every scene is as important as the scene itself. The scenes must be numbered, in sequential order, beginning with the number "one".

FOR EXAMPLE:

FADE IN:

1. EXTERIOR—WESTERN STREET—DAY

Western Street is enough of an indication to know it is a dirt road with wooden buildings, fronted by steps, hitching posts, a saloon, probably a jail, etc. The exact type of street will eventually be determined by the action and designed through the cooperative efforts of an art director, producer and director.

DAY or NIGHT is indicated for the same reason cited for EXT. (exterior) and INT. (interior). Unless indicated by the dialogue, the reference to time is not known. Also these are more important than just establishment of locale and time of day, for they provide the basis of the shooting schedule.

EXTERIOR or INTERIOR indicates the place around the settings. NIGHT or DAY is the time which is established after a transition only.

After establishing locale and setting, the next step is the CAMERA direction. It is also indicated in CAPS—such as LONG SHOT.

In the example below, the number indicating the scene appears opposite LONG SHOT. There is no specific rule stating that the scene number must appear opposite the phrase denoting the shooting location.

FOR EXAMPLE:

FADE IN:

EXT.—WESTERN STREET—DAY

1. LONG SHOT
The camera direction is indicated by the author only where it will assist his fellow craftsmen to understand the mood, where a dramatic point is made with a camera direction, or an essential plot point or a visual image is necessary.

The dialogue of the characters is indicated by their names in CAPS.

FOR EXAMPLE:

JANE:

. . . Ten-thirty and where is he, now?

The description of the character's attitudes and actions is usually placed in parentheses below the character's name.

FOR EXAMPLE:

JANE:
(irritated)

. . . Ten-thirty and where is he, now?

There is no need for CAPS to be used in the exposition after the main characters have been introduced and described.

3. Example: Step-Three
The Scenario

Step three is the expansion of step one, THE TREATMENT, and step two, THE BLOCKED OUTLINE of a simple story of JANE DOE.

FADE IN:

INT.—APARTMENT HOUSE KITCHEN—NIGHT

1. CLOSE SHOT—CLOCK

As the scene opens the CAMERA PULLS BACK to reveal the clock on the window ledge. It is ten-thirty. The CAMERA PULLS BACK more. We see in the reflection of the window, JANE DOE. She is middle-aged and haggard. OVER SCENE distant traffic noises are heard blending with the cry of a baby. Jane is doing the dishes.

JANE:
(irritated)

. . . Ten-thirty and where is he now?

2. MEDIUM SHOT—JANE
As she crosses to the stove we get a full picture of the tiny
kitchen.

> JANE:
> (to herself)

. . . And where does he go every night?

She crosses to the sink, then looks up at the clock.

3. REVERSE ANGLE—TOWARD JANE
Behind her we see the living room of the apartment. The room
is in great disarray.

> JANE:
> (continuing)

. . . For five years, I . . .

> (the sound of the door slamming)

Jane stiffens and wheels around, the CAMERA HOLDS on Jane.
In the background we see JOE through the living room into the
doorway of the kitchen.

4. CLOSE SHOT—JOE

> JOE
> Hello Jane . . . What's cookin'?

5. CLOSE SHOT—JANE

> JANE:
> (exploding)

What's cookin'? I'll tell you. You! That's what! We've
lived in this damn apartment for five years, now, and
all that time you have been floating from job to job.
What's more . . . there is someone else . . . I know it.

> (she pauses)

The CAMERA PULLS BACK as Jane pushes past Joe in a huff.
She disappears into the bedroom. Joe shouts after her.

> JOE
> Where do you think you're going?

> JANE:
> (from other room)

Joe, I've had it. I'm leaving you . . . It's no use.

INT.—BEDROOM—JANE

6. Jane is packing her suitcases. Through the open door behind her,
Joe passes by.

JANE:

This time you've gone too far. If it's sympathy you want
. . . go to her.

INT.—LIVING ROOM—JOE

7. Joe approaches a desk, opens the center drawer and gets out a
gun. He hesitates for a long moment as he looks towards the
bedroom. His lips tremble, his eyes glazed.

JOE
(to himself)

. . . You'll never leave me!

Now he starts toward the bedroom as he moves past the CAMERA.

The above example illustrates a possible method by which a single
sentence, expressing a story line, can be developed into a scenario.

THE CAMERA SHOT . . .

Note in the following scenario example, that the plotting of the
scene is indicated with the type of shot:

LONG SHOT — FULL SCREEN — WIDE ANGLE
— GROUP SHOT — MEDIUM SHOT — TWO SHOT
— CLOSE ANGLE — CLOSEUP — REVERSE
ANGLE — MOVING SHOT — ANOTHER ANGLE,
etc.

FOR EXAMPLE:

1. CLOSE—CORRIDOR, DEATH ROW

   THE CAMERA PULLS BACK as six men walk at a moderate
   pace down death row. Front and in the center is JOHNNY.
   He shows no emotion as he walks. He is dressed in regulation
   prison garb.

2. REVERSE ANGLE—THE GROUP

   THE CAMERA PULLS BACK as the group follows. To Johnny's
   right is the Warden. He glances occasionally at the doomed man
   as they walk slowly ahead.

3. CLOSE—JOHNNY'S FACE

   Johnny walks into a CLOSEUP. His eyes search the room as he
   snickers and shows a creased smile.

Transition indications, such as DISSOLVE, FADE, etc., are placed,
in CAPS, to the right of the page and usually three spaces below the
last portion of the exposition.

After the transition, we must re-establish EXTERIOR, or IN-
TERIOR, NIGHT, or DAY.

The opening of a place, a sequence, or time is ended by a transition. There is no repetition of exterior, interior, night or day until the transition.

FOR EXAMPLE:

FADE IN:

EXT.—TRAINING CAMP—NIGHT

1. MOVING SHOT

A moving shot through bright moonlight and deep shadow articulates an edge of a building, a tree, a part of the outdoor ring, a heavy sandbag slowly but barely swinging in the night wind. A wide window facing the clearing reveals CHARLEY WING, asleep, with the moonlight reflected on his face.

2. CLOSE SHOT—CHARLEY AS HE SLEEPS

He is struggling with a nightmare, fear etched on his face. Far off, a train whistle is heard. Charley wakes up, screaming.

DISSOLVE:

EXT.—PLACERVILLE STORE—NIGHT

3. MEDIUM SHOT

The store is a one-story building. A sign across the front reads: GENERAL MDSE. J. SINGLETON, PROP. A smaller sign reads: POST OFFICE. A wintry wind whistles through the dark deserted street. The CAMERA PANS to take in an old man, his white hair and beard stand out as he turns towards the opposite side of the street. This is OLD RANGER. He is joined by a tall, younger man, dressed in levis. His name is JED.

JED
(strong voice)

. . . How are you, Old Ranger?

The Old Ranger turns and walks away. Jed follows him and both men stop suddenly.

The Scenario—
The Scenario is a Liaison System

The sources of stories are infinite. Here is an example: A short news story appeared in the Los Angeles Times, March 8, 1959.

PAIR DISCOVER FAST WAY TO GET 'MARRIED'

LOUISVILLE, Ky., March 7 (AP)—A man and a woman entered Irwin Garber's pawn shop, purchased a wedding ring for $1, then told Garber: "Stand between us." Garber obeyed. The man put the ring on the woman's finger and proclaimed: "Now, we're married." Then the happy couple departed.

THE TREATMENT: (from the article)

A man and woman enter Garber's pawnshop and purchase a wedding ring for one dollar, then tell the pawnbroker to stand between them. Garber obeys. The man places the ring on the woman's finger, then proclaims, "Now we're hitched." Without delay, the happy couple depart from the store leaving the puzzled pawnbroker.

THE BLOCKED OUTLINE:

1. A man and woman enter a pawnshop.

2. The owner, Garber, sees them and goes to a counter as they approach.

3. Garber learns that the couple want to purchase a wedding ring.

4. He shows them a variety of rings. The man shakes his head as he is told prices.

5. As the man examines the rings, he selects one for one dollar.

6. The man pays Garber and tells him to stand between them.

7. Garber hands the ring to the man. The girl looks shy and smiles as the man places the ring on her finger. They kiss, then tell Garber this is their wedding ceremony. They leave in a hurry.
hurry.

8. Garber scratches his head in disbelief.

THE SEQUENCE:

The scenes (1), (2), (3), (4), (5), (6), (7) and (8) are arranged in series, each in different perspective. This is the entire sequence.

THE TRANSITION:

The scenes are arranged in continuing advancement. The couple leaves. The CAMERA SWINGS AND FOLLOWS Garber as he puts the dollar in the cash register. Suddenly he looks up, but the couple are gone. As a musical accent is heard off stage, he shakes his head in disbelief.

This scene promotes a change in events. Consequently, scene (8) becomes the climax of this sequence and the sequence DISSOLVES.

THE SCREENPLAY:

FADE IN:

EXT.—CITY STREET—DAY

1. FULL SHOT

THE CAMERA takes in a MAN and a young WOMAN walking

arm in arm as they approach a pawn shop. They hesitate for a moment as they look inside. He nudges her and they go into the shop.

INT.—PAWN SHOP—TOWARD ENTRANCE

2. The man and woman enter the shop. They are dressed simply, in country style. A bell sounds as they close the door. The man is smiling sheepishly as he looks at the shy, giggling woman.

3. REVERSE ANGLE—CLOSEUP—SIGN

A sign reads: IRWIN GARBER, PROP. THE CAMERA WIDENS THE SCENE revealing a smallish man who is busy appraising a piece of jewelry. He looks up and sees the couple.

GARBER
(with high-pitched voice)

. . . Ah! yes, yes, yes . . . come in. Now tell me, how can I help you?

MAN:

Wanna see whatcha got that looks like a weddin' ring . . . Don't need to be the fancy kind . . .

GARBER:

Of course . . . of course . . . I can tell right away, what you had in mind . . . yes, yes . . .

MAN:

You can?
(looks Garber over)

Then we come to the right place

Garber motions them towards the opposite end of the counter. The couple move awkwardly to follow as Garber directed.

4. MEDIUM SHOT—GROUP

THE CAMERA is behind Garber and favors the couple as they move into the frame. Garber takes a tray from the showcase below and reveals an array of rings.

GARBER

. . . Now here is one . . . a beauty! Solid gold . . . Just for your lovely lady . . . Let's try her size . . . I'll make it fit, sure . . .

The young woman raises her right hand and extends all her fingers. She looks at her man as she does this. She giggles and giggles. The man places his hand over her mouth to stop her giggling.

MAN

. . . How much?

GARBER

A bargain! Twenty dollars. You're lucky. I just marked
it down for you . . .

The man shakes his head, at the same time lowers the woman's
hand. Garber is quick and selects another ring. The woman extends all her fingers again.

GARBER

Well, now here is another bargain for you . . . a real buy!

Garber selects the index finger of the girl's left hand and tries to
place the ring on it. It won't go on. She takes it off and puts it on
her pinky finger. It fits.

GARBER
(quickly)

. . . Fifteen dollars!

The man shakes his head and sets the girl's hand down again.
Garber barely manages to retrieve his ring. He removes it from
her pinky finger.

MAN

Don't want nothin to do with so much gold in it.

Garber appears to be impatient as he looks the couple over.

5. REVERSE ANGLE—CLOSE—GARBER

Garber looks up from his glasses which tip his nose and sees the
man has turned his attention to a variety of costume jewelry rings.
A small sign reads: *Your Choice, $1.* The man points to a ring.

6. TWO SHOT—MAN, WOMAN

The angle is from Garber's point of view. The man smiles a broad,
toothless grin. Picks up a ring from the collection.

MAN

. . . Yup! rat chere tis'. We'll take it!

He fumbles a folded dollar bill out of his pocket and shoves it
into Garber's hand.

MAN
(continues)

Now, Mister pawn man, stand rat chere between us.

Garber does as he is told. The man arranges himself and the young woman on either side of Garber. The CAMERA PULLS BACK TO A WIDER ANGLE. The man forces the ring on the girl's finger, takes her in his arms and they kiss. The sound of it jars Garber.

7. ANOTHER ANGLE—THE GROUP

The couple separate and the man turns to Garber.

MAN

We're hitched! Thank ya for marrying us up . . . You're good cheap!

The tall, country man turns to the girl and takes her by the hand.

MAN

. . . We go tell yere pappy, then go back to the barn . . . Yowee!

He pulls the woman after him and they hurry out.

8. THE CAMERA SWINGS to GARBER. He looks at the wrinkled dollar bill in his hand. A MUSICAL ACCENT is heard. Garber looks up, puzzled, and shakes his head in disbelief. The scene FADES OUT:

EXAMPLES OF PHOTOGRAPHIC FORM

THE BOOK — THE SCENARIO — THE TELEPLAY

The following three examples indicate the application of all the principles of film writing heretofore mentioned. Note how a scene from the book interpreted by the film writer is translated into the scenario.

Note, also, how the scenario form differs from the teleplay. The teleplay form allows the director much more leeway in his shot selection. The shots indicated in the teleplay are hypothetical examples.

An excerpt from the novel, THE CHOSEN, has been selected to illustrate the techniques used in film writing. The excerpt is synopsized below.

The novel recounts the experiences of four men, who have been selected to study for the priesthood at a seminary. Of the four, only two are ultimately "chosen."

THE NOVEL: THE CHOSEN

Synopsis of an excerpt

Fifty, black-gowned figures piled into the lecture hall. For several minutes, there was complete confusion as each one scurried to find the chair assigned to him.

They put textbooks and notebooks down on the arms of their chairs, looked at each other trying to hide their uneasiness.

As a clock in the corridor began striking the hour, there advanced into the room a small, bespectacled professor in a much-worn cassock.

With toed-in, mincing steps, he went straight to the platform, deposited a book on the desk, faced the class and with downcast eyes and in a thin, uninflected voice, said a prayer.

As he finished, the professor's hand went inside the breast of his cassock and came forth with an astonishingly large, open-faced watch. He unhooked it carefully from the chain that held it, gave the stem a few quick turns, placed it precisely at the side of his book, and then looked up at the assembled, attentive, young men.

Father White's gaze had the simple, shy directness that is found in the very humble or the very wise.

The seminarians settled back in their chairs and awaited the professor's opening words. It was the first lecture in moral theology.

The announcement came from Father White that the text of his lecture would be conducted in Latin. However, questions might be asked in English if there was something not understood.

An awkward stillness pervaded the room. The professor folded one hand meekly over the other, smiled easily at the class.

The tension in the hall eased, and the lecture got under way. The first day's tension reflected on Steve Whelan's face. His eyebrows went up.

Seizing the book tightly in his big hands, he valiantly tried to hide his concern and plunged into the Latin morass.

THE SCENARIO: THE CHOSEN

Adapted by Arthur Ripley

The following scenes clearly indicate the manner by which one film writer has adapted the material of the novel synopsized above.

DISSOLVE TO:

INT.—SEMINARY—PHILOSOPHY CLASSROOM—MORNING

62. LONG SHOT

In the f.g. seated at a desk elevated on a platform with his back to the CAMERA, looking over some notes in the black, covered, looseleaf book is the figure of Father White, Prefect of Philosophy.

His white, wispy hair glistens in the early morning sunlight.

Before him, seated at their desks, are the fifty young men (first-year philosophers) whom we have already photographed in the dormitory, and whom we have heard Father White so humbly pray for the previous night.

It is their first class at St. John's. The first-day's tension is reflected on their faces.

63. MEDIUM—FATHER WHITE'S P.O.V.

Seated in the near f.g. in the rear of the class is Steve and, seated next to him, is the young seminarian who had watched him shave so carefully with a straight razor. The round-faced, pleasant young seminarian has written something in his notebook and, without taking his eyes off Father White, is holding it up against the arm rest of his seat for Steve to read.

64. CLOSE-UP—NOTEBOOK

This is a CLOSE INSERT of a notebook held in the young seminarian's hand. It reads:
Sometime would you teach me how to use a straight razor?

65. MEDIUM—FAVORING STEVE

Steve reacts to this strange request with a look of undisguised amazement. His neighbor smiles back at him benignly, hopefully. Whether or not this strange request is to be granted is left undecided for the moment, for the sudden, nervous clearing of throats announces that class is in session. Both Steve and his neighbor turn quickly to face Father White.

66. REVERSE—TOWARDS FATHER WHITE

For a moment Father White studies the faces before him. In a quiet, friendly voice he addresses them.

                    FATHER WHITE
Before we begin this first lecture on philosophy, gentlemen, I want to tell you how agreeably surprised I was to see the high scholastic records many of you had—before entering our seminary.
              (smiles encouragingly)
A gratifying large number of you have been honor students at your various schools. St. John's Seminary welcomes you.

67. FULL SHOT—FATHER WHITE'S P.O.V.

Father White, with his back to the CAMERA pauses to allow the class time to fully enjoy the compliment. They do. The reaction by most of the seminarians to these warm words of approval is instantaneous. Their faces beam with pride.

68. CLOSE SHOT—FATHER WHITE

There is still an encouraging, genial smile on Father White's face as he continues with his comments.

FATHER WHITE

. . . You will find that your subjects here at St. John will
require diligent and intensive study . . .
     (a note of warning creeps into his voice)

FATHER WHITE
(continues)
You may indeed, in the course of your intellectual ac-
tivity, be tempted to regard the primary purpose of your
being here, not as a sacard mission—and a vocation, but
as a training for a mere profession . . .
     (waits for the seriousness of his warning
          sink in, then continues)
Be reminded always, gentlemen, that your day here at
St. John's begins in chapel and ends in chapel, in prayer.
     (now smiles again)
And now to the task at hand.
He turns to a book in front of him, opens it.

69. FULL SHOT

THE CAMERA is on Father White. The seriousness of his warn-
ing has had its desired effect.
The black-cassocked figures sit motionless, waiting.

Father White looks up from the book he has been thumbing
through and, in a simple, direct voice, announces:

FATHER WHITE
The textbook we use is in Latin and all the lectures will
be conducted in Latin . . .
     (studies their faces)

Open your books, please . . . Page six, Chapter one.

70. CLOSE SHOT—STEVE

A look of slight panic and apprehension crosses Steve's face at
the announcement that the course will be conducted entirely in
Latin. It is immediately obvious that Steve doesn't consider himself much of a Latin student. And Father White's forthcoming pro-
nouncement, OVER THE SCENE, doesn't help matters.

FATHER WHITE
. . . You may ask questions in English—but all definitions
must be learned in Latin . . . Latin is concise and invariable and many of these definitions you will use again
later on—in your study of theology.

During this dialogue, coming OVER THE SCENE, Steve has
had a sudden bright hunch and has already acted upon it. He
has caught his neighbor's eye, written something rapidly in his
notebook and, at the moment, is flashing it at him beneath the
the arm rest of his chair.

71. CLOSE SHOT—NOTEBOOK

INSERT of notebook in Steve's hand. It reads:
Are you any good at Latin?

THE CAMERA pulls back taking in the seminarian peering at the note.

72. TWO SHOT—STEVE—SEMINARIAN

Steve's neighbor has already read Steve's note and is happily answering it. Guardedly he displays what he has written.

73. CLOSE SHOT—NOTEBOOK

INSERT of notebook in seminarian's hand. It reads:
Better than good. I'm a genius.

74. TWO SHOT—STEVE—SEMINARIAN

Steve, with controlled elation, reads the seminarian's note and quickly writes another one of his own. Again he flashes it.

75. CLOSE SHOT—NOTEBOOK

The INSERT of Steve's answering note reads, in large letters:
BROTHER—you have yourself a deal!

76. TWO SHOT—STEVE—SEMINARIAN

This business transaction by notes has been done very rapidly and both parties are elated over its consummation. They now get back to the business of listening to Father White's lecture.

77. LONG SHOT—MOVING

Father White is still seated at his desk facing the class with his back to the CAMERA. Completely ignoring his textbook, he begins his lecture.

The CAMERA MOVES past him toward the faces of the intent seminarians. It moves slowly past Dick, who, with book in hand and wrinkled brow, is painfully trying to follow the Latin text before him. As the CAMERA continues to move through the class, Father White's voice can be heard OVER THE SCENE.

FATHER WHITE
. . . The word philosophy is derived from the Greek—
and means the search after wisdom. It is defined as . . .
(recites in Latin)
Scientia retum ratione humana cogno scibilum per causas vel rationes ultimas naturali lumine comparata . . .

Father White's lecture is still coming OVER THE SCENE as the CAMERA MOVES INTO A CLOSE-UP of Marty.

78. EXTREME CLOSE UP—MARTY

    All thoughts of Alice seem to have been obliterated from his mind. With his Latin book before him, he follows intently every word Father White is saying.

79. REVERSE ANGLE—FROM MARTY'S P.O.V.

    The CAMERA points to Father White as he continues to recite his lecture as if it is from memory of doing it over and over.

80. WIDE ANGLE—THE CLASS OF SEMINARIANS

    They listen intently to Father White as THE CAMERA SLOWLY SCANS their faces.

81. CLOSE ANGLE—MARTY

    As we see Marty he appears to be in an intense mood, listening to Father White. We begin to hear the faint clang of street cars, taxi horns, the wail of an ambulance siren and the scene

                                                              DISSOLVES TO:

THE TELEPLAY: THE CHOSEN

    The following indicates the manner of adapting the material of the screenplay into a script for a live-television production as adapted by the authors for purposes of illustration herein.

PHILOSOPHY CLASSROOM

FATHER WHITE ENTERS THE CLASSROOM AND CROSSES TO THE PODIUM

                        FATHER WHITE ——— M/S

Before we begin this first lecture on philosophy, gentlemen, I want to tell you how agreeably surprised I was to see the high scholastic records many of you had before entering our seminary. (SMILE) A gratifyingly large number of you have been honor students at your various schools. St. John's Seminary welcomes you. We are very happy you are here. (PAUSE) You will find that your subjects here at St. John's will require dilligent and intensive study. You may indeed, in the course of your intellectual activity, be tempted to regard the primary purpose of your being here, not as a sacred mission, and a vocation, but as a training for a mere profession. (PAUSE) Be reminded always gentlemen, that your day here at St. John's begins in chapel and ends in chapel, in prayer. Now to the task at hand.

Handwritten margin notes:

X DISSOLVE

(2) PICK UP (FW) AT DOOR. PAN WITH HIM TO PODIUM

(1)

F/S (3)

L/S (1)

M/S (3)

F/S (1)

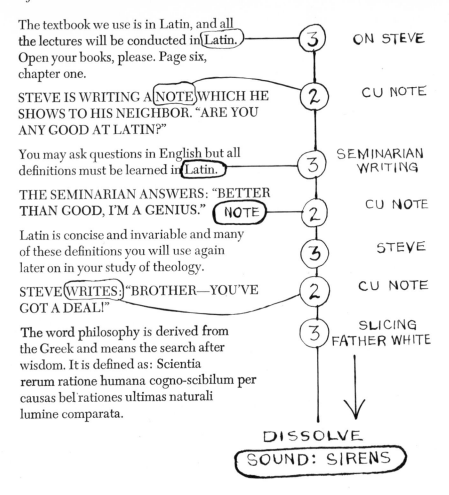

The textbook we use is in Latin, and all the lectures will be conducted in Latin. Open your books, please. Page six, chapter one.

③ ON STEVE

STEVE IS WRITING A NOTE WHICH HE SHOWS TO HIS NEIGHBOR. "ARE YOU ANY GOOD AT LATIN?"

② CU NOTE

You may ask questions in English but all definitions must be learned in Latin.

③ SEMINARIAN WRITING

THE SEMINARIAN ANSWERS: "BETTER THAN GOOD, I'M A GENIUS." NOTE

② CU NOTE

Latin is concise and invariable and many of these definitions you will use again later on in your study of theology.

③ STEVE

STEVE WRITES: "BROTHER—YOU'VE GOT A DEAL!"

② CU NOTE

The word philosophy is derived from the Greek and means the search after wisdom. It is defined as: Scientia rerum ratione humana cogno-scibilum per causas bel rationes ultimas naturali lumine comparata.

③ SLICING FATHER WHITE

DISSOLVE

SOUND: SIRENS

SELF ASSIGNMENT

Write a short scenario, or a portion thereof, using the forms and procedure previously established. The following points must be contained within the exercise:

 a. TRANSITION

 b. SHOTS and DESCRIPTION

 c. CAMERA DIRECTION

 d. The PLACE, the TIME, the CHARACTER

 e. ATMOSPHERE, MOOD, and LOCALE

 f. DIALOGUE

 g. TRANSITION to CHANGE, ENDING SEQUENCE

The following principles must be followed in the exercise:

 1. EXPOSITION: Preparation for action to take place within a a scene, sequence or story.

 2. CONTINUITY: How to extend story through advancement, action, motivation in sound, picture and transition.

 3. TRANSITION: Developing connection between divisions of a story through character, time and audience.

 4. TECHNICAL VALUES: Setting, time within which the story takes place, and environment.

 5. DRAMATIC VALUES: Arrangement of idea, situation, motivation, action and intensification.

 6. THE OPENING SCENE: Effective introduction of idea.

 7. SELECTION: Isolation of details for individual expression.

Chapter 10

THE USE OF PERSPECTIVE BY
FILM DIRECTOR AND
DIRECTOR OF PHOTOGRAPHY

... The Director's Proscenium ...
Significance of Cinematic Action
... The Director of Photography ...
Geography of a Camera Shot ...
... Working Demonstrations ... The
Creative Use of Lenses for the
Director ... Principles of Cine-
matic Composition ... The Effect-
ive Use of the Camera Angle ...

The Long Shot — Medium — Close Shot
The Angle: High — Low — Wide — Tight —
Reverse — The CAMERA PANS — Right —
Left — The CAMERA TILTS — Down — Up —
The CAMERA Moves In — Pulls Back —
Crosses — The CAMERA Takes In — Finds —
Points — Sweeps — Discloses etc., The CAM-
ERA is always focused on the emphasis of —

THE STORY . . .

Telling Story by Pictures—The Director's
Proscenium

The art of telling a story began with the primitive drawings in cave dwellings in prehistoric times. Next came story telling by pantomime, then the written word. These words are composed from alphabets which were originally pictures. Even today, the Chinese alphabet is a collection of pictures and ideas which form mental images.

Story telling is an art expressed in many forms. In the medium of the live theatre the story is dramatized on a stage framed by a proscenium, or in an area which is round, or on an arbitrarily confined level. In every case, the audience sees the action of the story, scene by scene, and act by act, as one. The physical limitations of this particular technique make it obvious that the story cannot be viewed in any other place, but only at a scheduled time in a setting or settings confined to that theatre area.

In the cinematic medium there exists a more flexible field of action. This allows the audience to find the story in a picture. The director, then, must have the ability to compose that picture into a story.

A director should tell his story honestly through all the craftsmanship at his disposal. He should know how to use his craft. He should do his work, in his own style in a variety of places, settings and environments, whether they be natural or specially designed according to the dictates of the story.

SIGNIFICANCE OF CINEMATIC ACTION

Effecting the Composition—
P.O.V. (Point of View)

From a simple blocking of the action, the line of vision develops what we want the audience to see. The process of selecting a point of view depends upon how much of the emotional and physical life experience is needed to embody the time and environment.

Situation—Story Part

A situation as it is placed or found in a story suggests a train of incidents. The cause of an action in a scene and the effect of it is embodied in the dramatic meaning.

The Angle—
The Story Takes the Same Position
As the Angle on the Screen

The selection of the angle in a shot reveals, by perspective, the significant moment which projects the cause of the action and the effect involved. The angle is what gives all things and images interest and meaning. The same thing taken from a different angle often gives a completely different meaning.

The changing viewpoint and the mobility of the camera provide a prime factor in developing the structure of a film story.

The Scene—
A Unit of Action

The IDEA in a unit of action in a story forms a link in a dramatic chain of events. When organized, the action becomes a SCENE.

A scene is marked by the length of time taken by the action. When the background and meaning changes, the scene gives way to another point of view. When the scene ends, another is established.

Usually, establishing a scene means a full view embracing the whole action. The angle from which the director sets the action, close or distant, and the sequences in which the successive actions are presented, determine how the audience views the story.

The Camera—
An Instrument of the Arts

The camera is a means by which the director makes a story move before an audience. It can capture a decisive instant or an exact moment in any setting or environment, far or near. As each picture is replaced by another, the story unfolds and addresses the audience—eyes, minds and emotions—thus creating a sense of reality. The audience is constantly participating in the story, no matter where the setting.

Cinematic Technique—
Recording Theme, Time, Place and Action

The cinematic technique is a part of an interpretive art; it is both creative and functional. The director in the cinematic technique and the camera are inseparable.

In the director's hands the camera is an accurate instrument which mirrors his concept of the story and the motivations for the actions he wishes to reveal to the audience. The camera can capture the vitality and variety with which people live. With perceptible detail, it can record the way a character thinks, feels and acts. In the cinematic technique, it is up to the director to capture the story in picture and words.

The camera itself is a mobile instrument. The director uses this mobility to focus audience attention. Such mobility can focus attention on either the emphasis of the story or on itself. When the audience realizes a camera is working, the meaning of the drama is disturbed. For the drama to be meaningful, the director must therefore dictate the extent of the camera movement.

Dramatic Constitution—
Reflecting Collective Action

The job of the director is to emphasize expressive story qualities, motivated by the theme, which result in an artistic pattern. This pattern is a reflection of the collective action in the entire film.

Process of Developing Dramatic Structure
Film Editing

Film editing is the art of selecting the emphasis in scenes which continue the theme from the preceding and succeeding actions. These actions are recorded by the camera on film.

The editing process employs the juxtaposition of scenes, thus creating a sequence of scenes. The film editor and the director work hand in hand to build the cinematic structure of the story in that the director must furnish the editor with complete and meaningful coverage of the actions and reactions of the emotional and physical elements in the story as portrayed by the characters. The sequences selected develop into a pattern of transitions which advance the story to its final climax.

Cinematic technique, unique to the film structure, enables the editor to compose the theme of the story which is edited from actions taken in two different places. The continuity of the scenes can be interpreted within the advancement of the action itself. The finally edited film, including all audible and transitional elements, forms the story on the screen. The story, the director, the actors, the editor and all technical aspects are now fused together to project a novel to be seen and heard, not to be told or read.

The View Finder—

A tool for the intuitive eye of the director. He lives with the concentration of spirit that he visualizes in the angle of a scene.

Artistic composition and technical perfection can be projected to the eye by the use of a view-finder. The view-finder masks the field of action for the director.

In composing the elements of a picture, it is important to view the staged field of action before a "take" is exposed for actual filming. The story reference lies within the frame; the preparation is outside.

A director must be a careful planner, deliberate, painstaking. His interpretation and point of view affect the success or failure of a production.

The viewing field of a picture should tell a story and appeal to the emotions. It should not contain any material unnecessary to the composition. The director should learn to work in constant cooperation with the director of photography, who, like the painter, strives for technical perfection and artistic composition.

The elements created within the picture composition should be arranged so that the advancement of each situation in a story can be played in continuous harmony.

The Film Director and the
Director of Photography—
present
The Story in a Picture . . .

A picture in series with other pictures must have the elements of discovery. It lives only with the life the creative directors put into it. The director soon finds that the story in a picture can be captured with artistic perspective that provokes thought, thus increasing the human eye interest. The pictures and thoughts then easily sketch the thoughts and control the emotions of the audience.

The point of view of the story, the theme, and the characters and their environment are the point of view a director-interpreter wishes the audience to assume. Its perspective of the drama becomes a creative responsibility which must never be diffused by superficial elements.

Directors Must Learn—

The Facts of Life in a Story . . .

An absolute necessity for effective visualization lies in the analysis, pre-planning and thorough concentration contained in picture composition.

The film director and the director of photography, (camerman) obtain a visualization of the drama which results in compatibility with other colleagues of the production team and total clarification to the audience.

The directors must learn to think in terms of motivation and continuity from scene to scene and sequence to sequence before film footage actually rolls, as it develops and as it ends. They must maintain the consistency in the characterization, the naturalness, mood and pace in the environment and the business of life-like contact in experience.

Each experience is a reflection of the situations found in life.

CREATIVE INTENTION

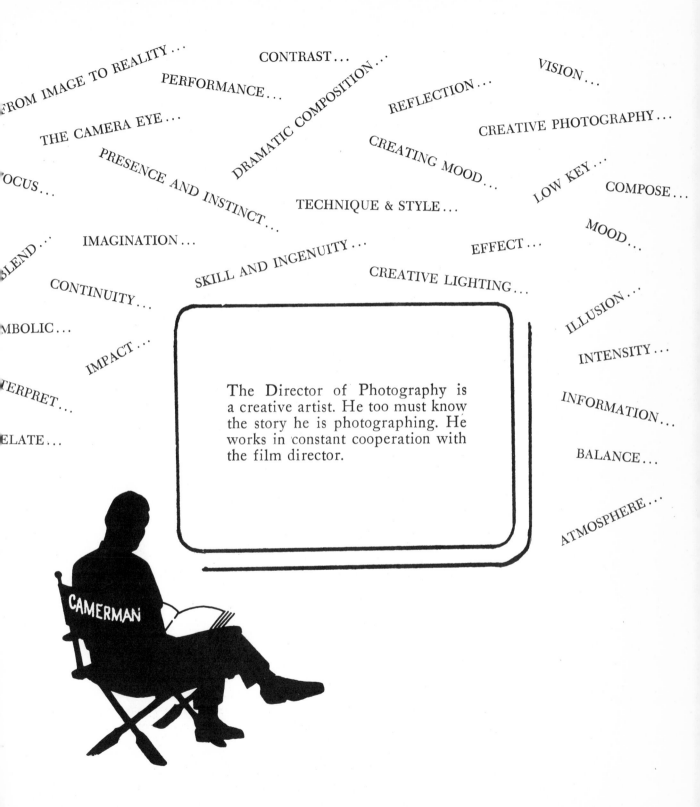

FROM IMAGE TO REALITY...   CONTRAST...   VISION...

PERFORMANCE...   DRAMATIC COMPOSITION...   REFLECTION...

THE CAMERA EYE...   CREATIVE PHOTOGRAPHY...

CREATING MOOD...

FOCUS...   PRESENCE AND INSTINCT...   LOW KEY...   COMPOSE...

TECHNIQUE & STYLE...

IMAGINATION...   MOOD...

BLEND...   SKILL AND INGENUITY...   EFFECT...

CONTINUITY...   CREATIVE LIGHTING...

SYMBOLIC...   ILLUSION...

IMPACT...   INTENSITY...

INTERPRET...   INFORMATION...

RELATE...   BALANCE...

ATMOSPHERE...

The Director of Photography is a creative artist. He too must know the story he is photographing. He works in constant cooperation with the film director.

CAMERMAN

THE DIRECTOR OF PHOTOGRAPHY (ASC)—A Creative Artist

A director of photography must know how to select the proper lenses and details which achieve the appropriate visual attention of the idea in motion. He must know how to use his imagination. Consequently, the director of photography will accomplish the correct meaning of the picture dictated to him by the film director.

Following are some important visual key points the director of photography must consider when he relates his own visualization of the drama to lighting and picture composition when a scene is blocked for action.

1. The order of preceding and succeeding attentions.
2. Picture motivation.
3. Emotional content.
4. Emphasis of the significance in the environment.
5. Imaginative detail.
6. Story relationship to the character.
7. Character relationship to the environment.
8. Means of getting visual balance and lighting balance.
9. What the audience will see.
10. What the audience will remember.

THE CAMERA IS MOBILE AND DRAMATIC . . .

In the director of photography's hands the camera is the chief instrument he learns to work with. The camera records the whole story.

The director of photography interprets for the film director's proscenium in the cinematic medium which lies within the flexible frameline of the camera. He is a creative artist who works with the space around the drama, for in this space lies the physical key of interpretive action.

GEOGRAPHY OF A CAMERA SHOT

A good film director understands, through his imagination, what a good camera shot means. He thinks visually and in terms of the position he wants his audience to take when they view the action. He should have a specific approach to the motivations for his actors and to the action in the story as the story develops, thus giving each picture, as it appears in the frame, specific significance.

TYPES OF CAMERA SHOTS THAT ARE BASIC— A BLUEPRINT FOR ACTION

The following illustrations (a), (b), (c), and (d), symbolic of the various types of shots, indicate the means by which the significance of a target or object of attention can be intensified visually for the audience.

(a) Long Shot

THE LONG SHOT

Somewhere in the long shot is the TARGET of attention, a target for the camera to focus upon or to emphasize. The target may be a person, an object, things or environment. A long shot is defined not only by how far, wide, long or deep it is, but by what the shot contains in relation to the story.

The long shot is usually a full screen view, used essentially as an establishing technique. The long shot is the orientation, referred to as the master shot. Pictorially, it is a wide and deep pattern. Emotionally, the shot promotes in the audience a certain expectation to follow.

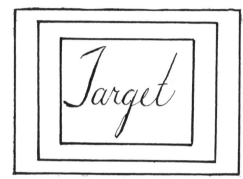

(b) Medium Shot

THE MEDIUM SHOT

This shot is the next step with which the director begins developing the significance of the target. The target begins to emerge as more significant than other details in the picture. It is a transitional shot which may lead forward to the close shot or backward to the long shot.

(c) Close Shot

THE CLOSE SHOT

In the close shot, the TARGET has emerged as the most significant in the picture. It is the most intimate camera shot of all and is sometimes called "tight" shot. The close shot is designed to underline or emphasize detail of people, or setting.

The close shot is used to accentuate and punctuate a scene, and show the characteristics of an object, as well as a person. The shot may also show a detail of the environment which might be necessary to the development of the story.

Emotionally, the close shot may reflect the action, thus allowing the audience to reflect with a character, or upon a situation. It may also be pointed toward a conclusion. The use of the close shot gives dramatic proportion and significance to time, place and person.

THE CLOSE-UP (**Extreme close view**)

The total appearance of the scene is intensified through the elimination of all the factors other than the TARGET itself. The close-up isolates the background to everything but what the audience is to see, feel and hear.

(d) Close-Up

In the close-up shot, the target has emerged as the most significant factor. It has been magnified in such a way as to intensify character, reaction or a relationship to a specific intention in the story.

The close-up, theoretically, is the end toward which the long shot points. It constitutes the fulfillment of expectation which began with the long shot. The audience will always look for the final development of a scene in a close-up. The TARGET can be made more significant with the addition of an audio element.

1. THE CLOSE VIEW . . .

The reference within the frame in (e) is full of realization as it is viewed.

The entire pictorial structure is then significantly seen and felt. In the picture to the left, the selection is more than a reference in the frame.

With dramatic use of the camera, this shot can either move in or move out.

(e)

The close-up is flexible in design and impresses a relationship of characters and spirit which is usually seen as something housed within the body of its possessor. It is dramatic.

2. THE MEDIUM VIEW . . .

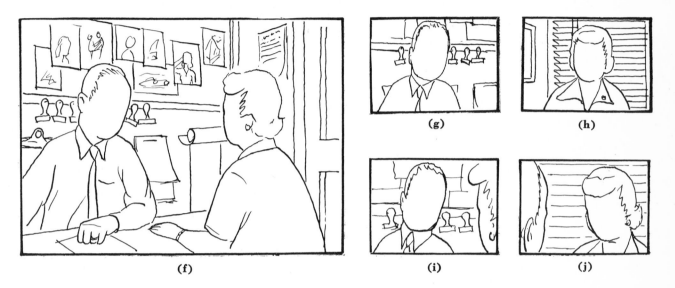

(f)   **(g)**   **(h)**   **(i)**   **(j)**

In the picture (f) above, a relationship is established between two individuals and between the individuals and their environment. In this picture, neither individuals nor details of the background have emerged as the most significant element of the picture. Therefore, a CUT is suggested by this relationship.

The CUT or change in (g), (h), (i), or (j), should be in juxtaposition with either the dialogue or the suggested reaction.

3. THE LONG VIEW—ESTABLISHING . . .

(k)

In illustration (k), the audience is oriented to area, locale, mood, atmosphere and a suggestion of the theme.

It also familiarizes them with the environment outside the frame, even as we move in close.

4. THE "MASTER" SHOT—
THE A,B,C, OF PICTURE COMPOSITION . . .

Attempting to tell the story without this initial long shot is much like bringing the audience in during the middle of a movie. The long shot or the master scene is known as the ABC of picture composition. The long shot represents a central reference point in the story.

When one sequence in one environment ends and another sequence in another environment is introduced, the master shot or long shot should be introduced to orient the audience.

The master shot establishes the nature and geography of the action in the scene. In it are contained all the important elements of the preceding and succeeding shots contained in the same sequence.

A series of master shots must be planned throughout the whole story in order that the audience can follow the theme, characters and the environment. The master shot is to the story what a backbone is to the skeleton. It is the base upon which the plot, theme and characterization rest.

5. THE "CUT"—CHANGE . . .

The cut is used to show the reactions of the individuals to one another or to a variety of attentions which have been established in a master shot. The cut differs from a pan in that the cut is made only for a change of emphasis in the story. If the attentions of the individuals in (f) were drawn to something outside the frame, not yet established, a pan would be suggested.

The director must remember that the development of the story does not depend solely upon the cuts and pans, for sometimes the story may develop only by allowing the action to play uninterrupted before the camera.

THE PAN and THE TILT

The pan is a horizontal movement of the camera and the tilt is a vertical movement of the camera. It is used to establish relationships, entrances, exits, or follow movement of actors. The pan can be used in place of a cut to show actors in conversation or to show reactions.

(1) The Pan

(m) **The Tilt**

The pan stimulates the normal covering action of the eye. At every given moment, the pan must maintain meaning and interest for the audience. The director must be certain that the space traversed by a pan or tilt, between objects of attention, is not so great that such movement becomes meaningless or uninteresting. Both the pan and the tilt can be used for emphasis or impact.

(n) **Trucking Shot**

TRUCKING SHOT

The trucking shot is a parallel movement of the camera to the action. It is used to follow an actor or actors or a moving object in direct profile. It can also be used in "follow-shots" such as following moving vehicles. The trucking shot is essentially used in large areas.

THE DOLLY SHOT

A dolly shot covers an area by moving in or pulling back of the camera. It is a movement in which the camera dollies back to include the rest of the scene which is outside the frame.

The reverse camera action could then be executed by dollying in to the most significant element of the picture.

(o) The Dolly Shot

To dolly-in on an actor, set or prop means to go forward with the camera on a mobile mount in a direct and smooth movement toward the target.

To dolly-back means to go backward with the camera from close shot, to medium, to long. The long is used to eliminate cuts to achieve a smooth, mounting emphasis or punctuation.

The dolly-in, in its best use, can represent the audience "moving in" for a better look at the most interesting points of the drama. Dollying-back gives the audience relief from an intimate scene to a wider perspective, and assists the director in building to another new dramatic high.

The movement of the dolly can often help build intensity or accent important points, either in dialogue or in connection with props, setting, or facial expressions and body movements of the actors themselves. The movement is also used to "lose" or "pick-up" actors or objects.

Dollying the camera should be used with utmost care and control. Too much movement often disturbs the drama, thus resulting in loss of attention. On the other hand, complete lack of movement might present the drama as less developed in the full cinematic technique.

PROCESS OF CHANGE—RELATED COMPOSITION . . .

All actions point to a transition in which the effective advancement or climax is reached.

Time is best expressed through transition which becomes a treatment devoted to change. Transition gives the audience time for reflection—time to return to the story between inter-connections. It provides a bridge between one sequence and another.

TRANSITIONAL UNITY . . .

In illustration (p), a young woman is alone in a room. The time is day. The theme is indicated by the letters and the photo of the soldier on the table. The calendar on the wall and the opened letter beside the young woman reveal that she is waiting for something important to happen.

(p)

The transition binds together an unlimited series of events into a meaningful unfolding of the story. Thus unity is accomplished in film through the transition.

"P" DISSOLVES TO "Q"

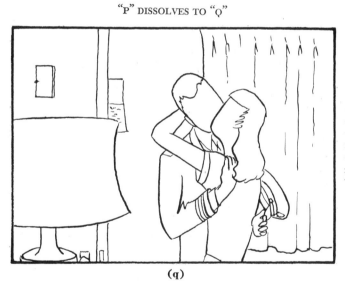

Illustration (q) is the transition of the scene above in (p). The room is the same. It is night. Now the young woman is in the arms of the soldier who was established in (p). There is a time change and a story change as the new character is introduced. A series of scenes (not indicated), have occurred between illustrations (p), and (q).

(q)

The transition from one shot, scene or sequence to another unifies the significant points of the drama and gives the film story continuity. The transition is a mechanical device designed for the audience.

The transition can be effected by the story, character, environment and time.

THE SEQUENCE . . .

A series of succeeding and preceding scenes in successive actions become united, through their juxtaposition, into a sequence of scenes usually called "sequences".

PURSUIT OF IDEA . . .

The pictorial framework of the story can be found in the master shot. The director must learn how to control his composition by dealing with the point of view, the breaking point and the resolving scene in a sequence.

When the action is to have significant meaning, the director should consider the following points:

1. What is it that establishes environment, character and theme?

2. What is it that develops the motivation of the story?

3. What picture content should be organized to reveal WHAT, WHEN and HOW significant it is to see, hear and feel?

The story in illustration (a) is established in a room as a woman stands before a dresser. She is crying as she looks at the photo in her hands.

The spectator has been orientated as to the setting and situation. This is the MASTER scene.

(a)

The director is now free to move in close on any aspect of the scene without confusing the audience. After the master shot has been established, the audience wants a closer look. Thus the director orients the audience with a master shot, then carefully selects parts of the scene which motivate the theme.

The next scene might show a close shot of the photo in her hand. The first expectancy of the audience has been satisfied; however, it wishes to know more.

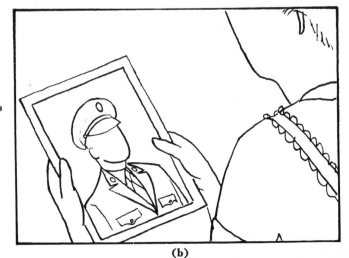

(b)

(c)

The next CUT, (c) might be the woman's face reacting to what she sees in the photo. There is something else behind the photo in her left hand that focuses our attention.

(d)

In (d) it is now conclusive that the telegram in her hand has a significant relationship to the photograph on the dresser.

This entire sequence might have been played in one master shot. However, it would lack the drama of exposing the theme through selection of emotional parts. These cuts might be presented in a different combination depending upon interpretation.

In a sequence, the master scene can appear in any order providing the relationship of the sequences has logic and meaning as they reach a climax.

Illustration (e) reveals the setting to be a cabin, deep in the woods. The ruggedness of the whole area suggests loneliness.

(e) Establishing Shot

In this cut (f) the details of the cabin stand out. The lack of activity furthers the mood of the scene. Our attention now focuses on the door as it opens cautiously. There is audience expectation as the figure at the door appears to be that of a small boy.

(f) Developing Shot

This illustration (g), shows the character of the little boy. His appearance and the environment complement each other. The story develops into a stronger pattern as tension builds by the way he moves.

(g) Significant Shot

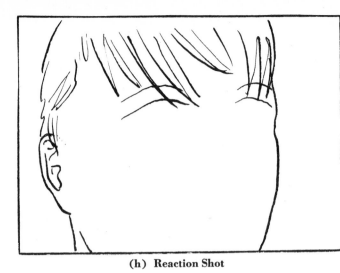

In illustration (h), we cut directly to the tense face of the boy. The audience feels the emotions of the character as it now sees his face. This close-up makes a strong point in the story. The audience now wants to know the reason for his reaction.

(h) Reaction Shot

The very next shot should expose the product, meaning and motivation of what the little boy sees, thus completing the sequence.

WORKING DEMONSTRATIONS

The following are suggested story ideas from which a motion picture sequence can be developed and blocked for the action and filming.

1. A rivalry between sisters flares into the open. A spinster school teacher suddenly fights desperately for marriage.

2. A study of a small town and some of the people in it. A new character is introduced whose personality sets off a chain of explosive reactions.

3. A train rolls into a small town station. A tall individual gets off. He has come home. The man has been pardoned from a life jail sentence. Waiting for him is his wife and another man.

4. A new school teacher takes over a classroom. The students are teen-agers, many of them belligerent and delinquent.

   Her brother, a student in the class, protects her from a small group of boys.

   He is a member of the group.

5. A young widow is informed by her physician that she is about to lose her eyesight. Her circumstances become desperate as she decides to leave her eight-year-old son in an orphanage.

5a. Years later, now re-married, well-to-do, and with her eyesight partially restored, she locates the boy, but discovers that he, too, is blind.

6. This is opening night for Kathy's first Broadway appearance. Since she came to New York, a man, many years her senior,

has fallen in love with her. The man has sponsored Kathy's schooling as an actress. Her fiancé, her own age, has arrived, determined to take her home.

7. The door of a construction engineer's office bursts open. A mother, whose son has just been crushed to death by one of the huge winches, stands there. It is the company's fault.

8. A bachelor employs a pretty girl named Greta as a housekeeper. She proves so attractive to him that he falls madly in love with her. He proposes marriage. She consents with one stipulation— that he put all his savings in her name.

9. A young lady, suffering from claustrophobia, enters an elevator. She is the only passenger. The operator has just recently been released from a mental institution. They are on their way up, when suddenly, the elevator stops between floors. The power is off. The elevator is dark.

10. Jail was a happy place today for Mr. and Mrs. James Doe and three of their children. They were together again under the same roof for the first time in three years. During those years, Doe twice was sentenced to die in the electric chair for the slaying of a local merchant. His wife, Irene, struggled to keep the family together and firmly believed her husband innocent. The man really guilty was found and confessed.

THE CREATIVE USE OF LENSES FOR THE DIRECTOR

LENSES—TO CREATE VISUAL COMMUNICATION . . .

Lenses have different values from the eyes. The camera discovers significance in things which seem unimportant. It also may be deficient in the areas where the eye is attracted psychologically.

The camera teaches a new way of observing the commonplace and enriches the viable world of infinite detail. The creative use of lenses stresses the capabilities to capture the spontaneity of a subject, idea or event and combine it with an ever effective sense of composition.

The properties of lenses transmit the subtle and direct use of photography to convey, inform and entertain.

THE LENS SYSTEM—AID TO THE DIRECTOR'S CREATIVITY.
SELECTION FOR STORY DEVELOPMENT.

A lens system is enclosed in a case and by its properties transmits to a recording device. A lens design is used to compose and build images. It can depict an isolated part without showing the total relationship to the whole peripheral frame of reference. A specific integral part can communicate the emphasis of a scene through and by a lens.

Thus, a lens is more than glass and design. It can either take in more or less detail than the naked eye and magnify it so it becomes significant in the picture which is presented to the audience.

The lens can take in an area much greater than that of the area of acceptance. It then presents that area in a four to three ratio for standard projection.

The lens is the eye of the camera. The director changes lenses in order to take in details of a scene he wishes to show. The demands of the story as interpreted by the director dictate the choice of lenses. The choice of lenses must then be motivated as the editing of the action.

(a)

In illustration (a), the director has selected the point of focus for the audience. This then indicates that through creative use of lenses the director has control over the audience's power of selectivity.

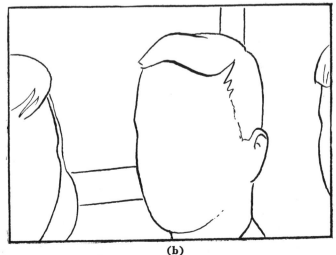

(b)

In illustration (b), the focal length of the lens has been increased from that used in illustration (a).

By this change, the director has increased concentration of the audience on the object of attention.

As you look at a picture, a concentration on some object, thing, image or thought may change your focus of attention from the overall picture to that specific object, thing, image or thought.

In doing so, you are utilizing your power of selectivity, a precious gift the camera does not possess, for the lens selects only the object you select for it, and its changing focus is a mechanical process.

The lens thus affords a method by which to gain insight into character, setting, locale and mood according to the demand of story development. It takes in only what the director wants the audience to see.

A wide-angle lens, for instance, can take in a larger area than could be accepted by the human eye, but can present it in such perspective that the human eye can accept it.

A narrow-angle lens, on the other hand, can take in a small portion of the area of acceptance and magnify it in such a way as to present details of this small area which would be noticed only slightly by the audience.

The director may wish to sacrifice depth in a picture composition in order to emphasize certain details necessary to story development. These details otherwise might be lost if depth were maintained.

The director may wish to sacrifice something else in order to achieve a feeling of great space.

He may wish to sacrifice a realistic point of view in order to take in many details which are necessary to story development. A good film director can sense what the power of emphasis will do and selects the exact note of reference in tune with the story in his pictorial composition.

The director chooses appropriate lenses to meet the demands of the story, much as the conductor blends the tones of the various instruments into a harmonious symphonic whole.

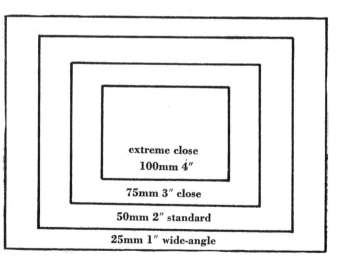

The director must harness the camera to his creative mind and not his mind to the camera. A good film director does not permit the spectator to look at a scene at random. He leads the eye from detail to detail and is able to place the emphasis of attention on the story in every photographed frame.

The film director regards the camera and its lenses just as the artist regards his palette, brushes and colors. The screen is the director's canvas so that, with the multitude of equipment, combined with the arts allied to the cinematic medium, his creation shall appear on it.

THE BASIC LENSES—STANDARD, WIDE-ANGLE AND LONG . . .

35mm	16mm	TV
Standard Lenses		
50mm	25mm	50mm
40mm	22mm	
Wide-Angle Lenses		
20mm	10mm	35mm
25mm	15mm	
35mm	20mm	
Long Focus Lenses		
75mm	40mm	90mm
100mm	50mm	135mm
150mm	75mm	

In addition to fixed lenses there are wide variety of 200m-type lenses with various 200m ranges. One common type has a range from 40 to 400mm (1.6 to 16 inches). This is known as a 10-1 zoom range.

THE CAMERAMAN AND THE LENS—IN TERMS OF STORY . . .

The cameraman knows that the lens has a different standard of values from the eye. It also may be deficient in those areas where the eye is attracted psychologically. He knows that the lens can reflect a concentration on the theme, an idea, a character. He knows that a picture is not meant only to be seen, but also to be understood.

The cameraman depends upon the director to "call the signals". The director must interpret the story for the cameraman. The cameraman's job is to know how to achieve that interpretation.

The cameraman (director of photography) as a creative artist, through lenses, lighting, pictorial perspective and his materials, achieves the interpretation of the story for an audience.

LENSES—PROPORTION AND PERSPECTIVE AS EFFECTED BY FOCAL LENGTH . . .

These illustrations show how proportion and perspective are effected by the focal length of the lens.

In this scene the lens was changed and the camera was moved to keep the image of the man the same size in the frame.

Notice the exaggerated perspective. Not only does the background loom closer, but the proportion of the figure also changes.

THE AUDIENCE AND THE LENS
—FOCUS ON EMPHASIS AND ATTENTION . . .

A well-composed picture will focus the eye upon the object of attention or target. If the attention is properly focused, the illusion of reality is sustained and the audience participates in the story rather than merely looks on.

PRINCIPLES OF CINEMATIC COMPOSITION

PICTORIAL DESIGN . . .

The key to cinematic composition lies not only in the arrangement of the elements of a picture, but also in the arrangement of the physical and emotional reactions of the characters who are followed by the camera.

Pictorial design is form in motion. It has function, awareness of purpose and reason in design. When applying the objective principles of picture composition, the director, in staging and blocking the action, must consider the factors of SITUATION, CONTINUITY and BALANCE. These must be arranged in the composition so that the images, as they are discovered by the audience, will suggest an emotional attitude in the dramatic nature of the situation without the use of dialogue. Some of the important elements which govern pictorial design are: (a) SELECTION, (b) DEFINITION, (c) ENVIRONMENT, (d) MOTIVATION, (e) PARALLEL EMPHASIS, (f) SYNCHRONIZATION, and (g) STYLE.

SELECTION—WHAT, HOW, WHEN, IN A SCENE . . .

Selection deals with getting the audience's attention and holding it as the sequence is developed. Selection deals with the director's concern of WHAT to begin with, HOW to advance the action and WHEN to conclude.

By way of example, are the following illustrations, beginning with (a) used with this theme: A man, housebound, is awaiting the arrival of another man who has in his possession certain documents which he has been using for extortion. The director then begins his sequence by selecting the best possible "cut", or camera angle which will begin the action and help advance it, thus moving it toward a dramatic conclusion. As each director has his own style, any combination of the illustrations, (a), (b), (c), (d) and (e) may be used, such as the combination of (a), (c), (b), (d), and (e), etc.

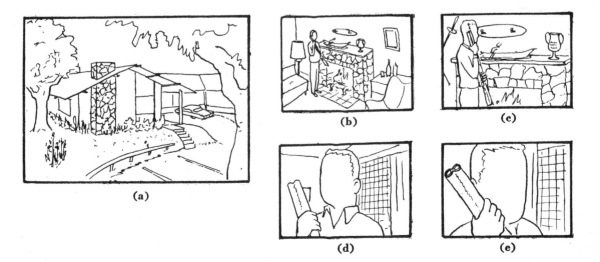

(a)   (b)   (c)   (d)   (e)

DEFINITION—EMOTIONAL OUTLINE . . .

Definition is a point of view, in which the focus of attention defines the substance from the environment.

A picture is not only defined by its outline but by the force of the drama in it. Light, shadow, atmosphere and mood help in the visual effect.

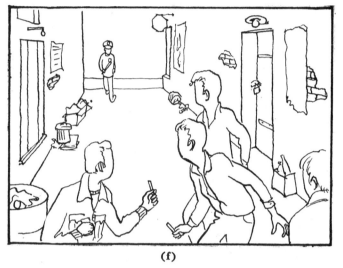

(f)

Illustration (f), above, offers only a focus of attention, without the use of light and shadow.

It offers environment and physical characteristics only.

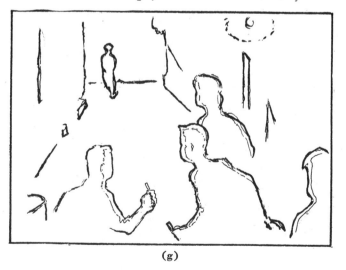

(g)

By way of contrast, illustration (g) now contains all the elements necessary to produce the desired visual effect. Light, shadow, atmosphere and mood have now been fused with the environment, creating the full force of the drama. Definition is an emotional element of what the eye sees.

ENVIRONMENT—BACKGROUND AND FOREGROUND . . .

Environment deals with the entire locale, mood, atmosphere and setting. In principle, it is where the character lives at all times during the drama. The background relates to the elements behind the actor in action. The foreground dictates the needs of the design and properties necessary for emphasis of the elements in front of the actor.

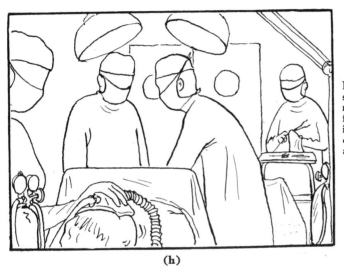

Illustration (h) shows a master scene, a patient in an operating room. The background and foreground environment are clearly indicated; both lend to the total environmental effect and atmosphere of the picture.

(h)

MOTIVATION—STORY IMPRESSION FOLLOWING ACTION . . .

Motivation is found in the reason and meaning for considering the physical situation and character complex. The meaning and reason in the design of the visual elements will form the thought which aids in developing the following action.

Each character in a scene must have specific motivation. For example, in illustration (i), the man with the gun has been "motivated" to kill the character with the brief case. The figure restraining the man with the gun has been "motivated" to get the brief case without killing. The character with the brief case is transporting secret documents to his office. These documents are the basic motivation for the presence of the three men.

(i)

PARALLEL EMPHASIS—INTEREST AND
ADVANCEMENT OF THE THEME . . .

Parallel emphasis is found and arranged in the drama to intensify the elements of attention. It can be achieved in one scene, or in several scenes, with one or many characters in different places, as long as the theme relates to a continuous story meaning. By juxtaposition of the scenes, the situation is held in continuous sequence.

(j)

Illustrations (j) and (k) concern different characters in different places. The woman is telephoning the doctor concerning her husband who is ill. The doctor receives the call.

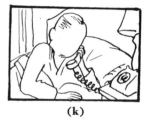

(k)

SYNCHRONIZATION—VISUAL AND AUDIBLE UNITY . . .

Synchronization is the marriage of picture and sound, thus complementing reason, meaning and reaction.

Synchronization results in life-like experience to the characters in the drama and to the audience.

Synchronization in illustration (l) is realized in this full view of a scene, showing the characters engaged in warfare.

Without synchronization, the impact would not affect the emotions.

(l)

STYLE—INDIVIDUALITY IN ARTIST MEANS . . .

Style is exemplified in the spirit of the artist. It is determined by the point of view by which a story is interpreted. Style is reflected by the director's particular way of working.

THE EFFECTIVE USE OF THE CAMERA ANGLE

THE "V"—A METHOD OF VIEWING THE ACTION . . .

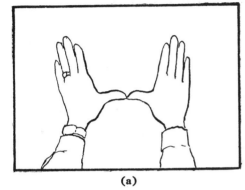

(a)

FRAMING WITH HANDS

Often when a director blocks a scene, he will hold his hands with the palms facing out, his thumbs touching. He views the action through the space between the index fingers, (a), the frame of reference resembling that of the frame-line in a picture.

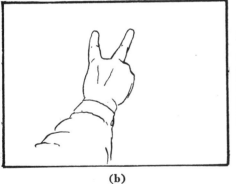

(b)

FRAMING WITH THE "V"

A method for indicating camera placement and a desired angle of the "shot" is to extend your hand forward, index and middle fingers separated and extended, projecting toward an area where the action is to take place.

The two methods, illustrated above, are purely mechanical means for blocking a scene and are only an aid to the director. He may also use the view-finder in lining-up a "shot." Some directors have trained themselves to such a degree that when observing a scene, they automatically picture a frame around that scene.

Regardless of which method the director uses, he must combine it with his "power of idea" in order to create a scene in which the drama is fully realized.

IMAGINATION—POWER OF IDEA . . .

Imagination is the key to creative thinking. Imagination is the primary consideration not only in the selective and development of the camera angle, but also in the entire drama. Imagination is putting thought and idea into effective use.

A primary attribute the director should possess is the ability to use the power of his imagination. Every good director must apply this power to his working principles, which enables him to organize a scene with the proper cinematic technique.

The organization of a scene deals with many logical relationships—setting, people, design and the technical crafts. The components of the story must be organized in the staging area to the degree that proper esthetic balance is achieved. This is expressed through the emotional design of the environment and the relationships of the characters both to the environment and each other.

As the director "sets up" for the camera, he should use his imagination in expressing the story for what the camera should see and for the type of shot that will best develop the story.

The camera is the liaison between story and screen. The director should endow the camera with human sight in order to translate story into sound, dialogue and picture. The camera, then, is the audience. It provides an intimate insight into a character or an environment.

THE CHANGING ANGLE—CAMERA EXPRESSION . . .

In this illustration (c), a change is dictated by the story, in that the figure in the foreground will turn to the figure in the background—thus the director is required to show close-ups of both individuals.

(c)

A change in angle is usually used to show the reactions of individuals to one another or a variety of attentions which have been established in a master shot. The change promotes intensification in visual story building. Change, as a definite approach to the action, interconnects dialogue, contrasts, conflict and emotion. Change promotes a combination of attentions into a moving form of the story. Changes are dictated by story development. Change must have control. The director must remember that the development of the story does not depend solely upon changes, but that the story may develop best by allowing the action to play.

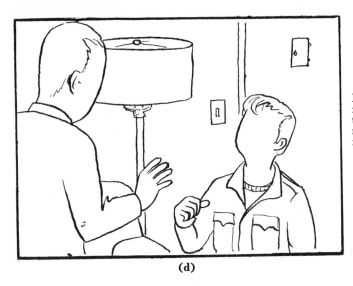

(d)

In this illustration (d), the director feels the change dictated to him through the story development—requiring a close-up of the father's face as he reacts to his son's story.

CAUSE, EFFECT AND CHANGE . . .

Following is an illustration of a master scene in which cause, effect and change takes place.

(e)

A door opens and a man enters. He inhales as he closes the door.

He sees his young son smoking a cigarette. The boy sees his father and tries to hide the evidence. The father approaches the boy.

1. THE ACTION—The door opens—the father enters the room and inhales—he closes the door behind him.

2. THE CAUSE—The young boy is smoking a cigarette. The father reacts to what he sees.

3. THE EFFECT—The boy tries to hide the evidence and the father moves to him.

Cause stimulates motivation; effect is a part of that motivation and change is the result.

4. CHANGE AND BREAKING POINTS OF THE SCENES (d),
(e) and (f).

The first change of view is to what the father sees.
The second is to the boy's reaction.
The third change is to the whole action between the boy and his
father.
The entire setting can be established as we see the action. The scene
can draw near or expand in FULL VIEW as the action concentrates
into one area.

5. EXAMPLE FROM THE SCREEN STORY: "THE REBEL".

FADE IN:

EXT.—SPANISH ENCAMPMENT—NIGHT

1. FULL SHOT—MOVING

As the scene opens, we see a supply wagon located near a cluster
of trees. To the side of the wagon a guard is dozing, his head
resting on the barrel of his rifle. On the other side of the wagon,
a lookout is standing. Suddenly he spots something on the ground.

The story in screenplay form is illustrated above. The scene below
is an interpretation of that opening "shot".
This is the ESTABLISHING or MASTER "shot". In it, the environment is "established." Now the CAMERA is ready to transform the
story into a "life-like" experience on film.

(f) The Master Shot

PUNCTUATING THE FILM . . .

Just as a sentence is punctuated, so is a film. It has commas, semi-colons, exclamation points, periods, etc.

The commonest are:

THE CUT. (Cut-aways) (cut-ins) When one shot in a scene swiftly replaces another, it pushes the action forward.

THE DISSOLVE. (Lap-dissolves) (superimposures) One shot begins to fade out as another fades in over it. This is used to indicate either a short lapse of time or a change of place within a series of closely related scenes. The dissolve is similar to the scene curtain used to separate changes of locale during an act of a play.

THE FADE. The scene grows darker and darker, and out of blackness a new scene slowly appears.

Fading out and fading in is a signal that a sequence of scenes is finished; a major development in the plot has come to an end. The fade is similar to the act curtain in a play.

MOOD—ENVIRONMENT—ATMOSPHERE . . .

1. Mood

MOOD is an emotional element. Like the story, mood has a beginning, middle and an end.

Mood must be developed and it must come to a conclusion. In creating a mood, one cannot forget the influences of both atmosphere and environment, for mood cannot exist without contrast and conflict.

Like the action of the actors, mood needs definition, contrasts and motivation. Mood cannot exist by itself or without support. Alone, it cannot convey a meaning, but a meaning can be conveyed through the use of mood if it is supported by the other elements which make up the entire composition.

2. Environment

ENVIRONMENT is that which surrounds. It supports the mood. It is not an intangible. It can be seen and must be seen, yet it too, like mood, cannot exist alone.

Environment affects each picture in a different way, consequently it needs support from the story as much as it supports the story: The drabness of a hallway in a tenement section can be dispelled easily by children's laughter, and yet the same drabness can be emphasized by the quiet sobbing of a young woman. In each case the environment is the same, supporting and conveying a meaning, a different mood.

3. Atmosphere

ATMOSPHERE is an intangible growing out of the mood, environment and action of a scene. It is the sub-total of story points.

It is the necessary by-product of the story without which the story cannot exist.

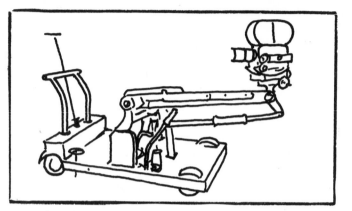

The CAMERA is a Mobile Instrument of the Arts

The CAMERA MOVES with . . . The CAMERA and the man come to a halt . . . The CAMERA pulls back to a wider angle to include . . . As the CAMERA is directly on . . . The CAMERA moves into a CLOSER ANGLE of the two men, then pulls away . . . The CAMERA moves into a big head close-up . . . The CAMERA moves forward, then upward, past the building.

The CAMERA pulls back to a full shot . . . The character walks into a close-up . . . The CAMERA moves through the darkness . . . When the dissolve clears, we are in a close-up of . . . During the dialogue, the CAMERA pulls back to a medium.

The CAMERA is now moving as . . . In a low CAMERA set-up, we are . . . The CAMERA pans away . . . On these words, the CAMERA moves past . . . The CAMERA, etc.

✿   ✿   ✿

Chapter 11

THE DIRECTOR'S CREATIVE INTENTION

...His Working Relationships...
to WRITER...ACTOR...TECHNICIAN
...AUDIENCE...The Actor
and the Cinematic Technique...
...Artistic Problems—Expressive Control...

THE DIRECTOR'S CREATIVE INTENTION

HIS WORKING RELATIONSHIPS TO—WRITER—ACTOR—TECHNICIAN—AUDIENCE

DIRECTOR-WRITER RELATIONSHIP

The writer is considered the original creator. He works with thoughts and speech. His professional skill and function are putting the "pen to will".

The director is the chief interpreter of a story and from it he extracts a maximum amount of expression. He possesses the basic control over the cast and technical interpreters.

A director should be capable of expressing, through the visual and audible structure of the film media, a dramatic sense of projected qualities. He must be objective in thought and action with regard to the personal emotions of his fellow artists. He is the liaison between the story and the audience.

The most important function of a director is to analyze the basic properties of the story. He must examine it for melodrama, drama, comedy, farce, tragedy or documentary qualities.

For example, if the plot dominates the character, as it does in melodrama and farce, the director must find an approach for his interpretation. This approach would differ from a plot in which the character dominates, such as in tragedy. The director functions adequately only if his analysis and approach determine how he expresses his decisions and interpretations to an audience.

DIRECTOR AND THE PLAYWRIGHT—HAND TO HAND ARTISTS

The author is the first artist, in sequence, through whom thought and imagination are developed into a story treatment.

After the author has written the story, he turns it over to the interpreters—producers, directors, actors, scenic designers, technicians and craftsmen.

Writing is more than putting words together. It is putting *ideas* together. This requires creative analysis. The writer must create and analyze a plot in terms of theme and characterization, and project this analysis into a story in an environment and setting.

It is up to the director to discover the key to the action of the story. The writer's thoughts must reach the director's imagination. The significant element in the director's thinking must come alive in order to provide the visual and audible effects used in staging the story before the cameras.

The director must uncover every possible relevance regarding the environment and the characters in it. He organizes his material from what the writer has given him. His direction is keyed to the writer's thoughts.

A director interprets visual contrasts from the screenplay. If the characters move, there must be proper motivation for the movement. If they don't, then the director should consider the motivation for a reaction.

The writer's research and creative process are expressed in his story. It is up to the director to find the material and the terms which will enable him to translate the action into film composition.

The relationship between director and writer varies with the demands of the story, the character development and the requirements of the production. The writer and director often work together to get to the heart of a situation in order to create proper character and story development.

In television film and live production, character development is a difficult problem. It is difficult to properly develop a character in "clock-timed" production. This is less of a problem for longer shows, however, but the television writer and director still do not have the time the screen writer or the playwright has.

The television writer relies more fully upon dialogue than upon broad action. The director should remember that the dialogue in a teleplay keys the action, motivation, emphasis and transitions. The writer must remember that both sound and dialogue must have logical continuity in the development of the story.

The writer is an artist-architect of words; the film director is an artist-engineer of movement who develops the emotional qualities of a story. The writer's thoughts and a director's point of view, together, can shape the story into a film form for the audience.

The material supporting theme, plot, and characterization involves the emotional content of mood and atmosphere the writer expresses in his script.

THE CREATIVE TEAM . . .

The relationship of the creative team, comprised of the director and writer, can be likened to the combination of a winning catcher and pitcher on a baseball team.

The film editor is the "creative team" manager, the actors are the team players and the producers are the trainers.

Instead of winning a ball game, the "creative team" wins the audience.

In the commercial sense, a good story, well directed and carefully produced, is a "pennant winner".

DIRECTOR-WRITER COMBINATION

Both the director and the writer must realize the need for each other's representation. Both artists interpret the story's time and design to the audience. The creative team of artists designs the action, the enjoyment, the knowledge, the experience and the story's intent to entertain an audience.

. . . THE DIRECTOR-ACTOR RELATIONSHIP

The above symbolic illustration is translated in the following manner:

The chair is the director—the fire is the actor—the logs and water are guidance: The logs—information—the water—control. The surrounding area is the entire production.

The flame of the actor is guided and controlled by the director who controls the proper temperature in surrounding areas. Without the sensitivity and control of the director, the fire would either dwindle and go out (in which case the surrounding area would go cold), or it would blaze out of control and destroy the entire production.

One of the most important members of a director's production team is the actor. Through him are motivated the great variables in the telling of the drama.

There is a link between how the director works—from the words of the writer as he writes—to that which will be interpreted by the actor. The actor's artistry arises more from pantomime than words.

The actor expresses the action of the story. He must be "pulled" into the representational environment by which he is surrounded. He must relate himself psychologically to the illusory world of walls, windows and doors. Moreover, he must distinguish between his own personality and that of the character he is portraying.

The reality and believability of the performance depends entirely upon the acceptance by the audience of the emotions displayed by the actor. It is this representational plane of performance which establishes rapport and empathy between stage and auditorium—between the frame-line and the audience.

The director begins fitting the actor to his role before actually meeting him in person. The director will determine what demands the script makes upon the character, and how the character's thoughts, movements and reactions should be interpreted.

The expressiveness of the actor is stimulated by the director. The actor's capacity to give a proper impression will depend upon what given meanings motivate his senses. The character needs to be logically impressed before the actor can clearly express himself. This can be accomplished through contrast, mood, sound, effects and action.

The actor senses proper motivation and he looks to the director to project the sustained conception of his character through such motivation.

CONTROL . . .

The control of a character's actions is influenced by the definition of the situation. The director must stimulate the "character role" in the actor, and render profile thoughts which drive his speech into action— and reaction. The director should convey only that information which will assist the actor in interpreting logical action in order that he can correctly respond to the situation and environment.

The individual artist depends upon the facts given him by his director so they may lead him to affect a specific impression. To stimulate his emotion and actions, the actor looks to the words and thoughts in the scenario. These come from inner emotions. The motivations should allow the actor to move freely and, at the same time, reveal the way he thinks and feels.

The actor must have more than dialogue—he must be able to use his feelings so those around him, as well as the audience, are constantly aware of his presence. He must be given reasons for his emotions.

AS THE ACTOR WORKS . . .

In following direction, the actor must, at the same time, exercise control of his characterization. He must be careful not merely to "act" his role (the result would be superficial at best). The role should be played naturally and in a life-like manner.

His performance must appear credible—believable within the frame of reference of the scene or story. If the actor has credibly created his role, the audience loses sight of the actor, per se, and sees the character whom the actor is portraying.

THE DIRECTOR CONTROLS . . .

A director controls an actor's movement, which must be expressive. The director must not stage meaninglessly. Artificial expression on the part of the actor will result in "hamming" instead of playing and living the character in a convincing manner. The actor's role must grow naturally. The director's responsibility is to guide the actor and motivate the situations and actions involving him to logical growth. These are important, from story point of view, both to the director and the audience.

EXPRESSIVE TIMING . . .

The facts governing an actor's control of communication depends upon his timing and how the director will effect the change of perspective to what is seen, heard, felt and understood by both the actor and the audience.

For example, a bride notes the reaction to her first meal served to her husband. She smiles politely as he, in turn, claims respectfully to like what he is eating. At the same time, she notes the rapidity and the eagerness with which he eats—the facial expressions in between bites—his shying away from reacting obviously.

There is a constant interaction affecting the transmission of reason, meaning and reaction as the director motivates and stages the actors. The director must be consistent in this regard.

THE ACTOR AND THE CINEMATIC TECHNIQUE

Because of shooting and working schedules characteristic of film production, scenes are generally shot out of sequence. All scenes in one place and setting will be exposed at the same time. Shooting may begin in the middle of the story, at the end of it, or even at the beginning. Consequently, the director in film has a greater responsibility than in other media for the consistency and continuity of the actor's performance.

The actor depends upon the director to fit him into the story continuity at all times. Only the director and the film editor will know the outcome of a scene, its juxtaposition and the advancement of the story. What the actor does at one moment must match his exact movements at the next.

A character may be conceived with imagination and his relationship to other characters may be planned with action. Yet, if the director does not motivate actions which promote contrasts, suspense and impelling drives, then he has failed in his responsibilities to the actor. The director must also match body positions and screen angles so that the actor will fit into the continuity pattern from one scene to the next, otherwise the scenes may end "on the cutting room floor".

A good actor must have a capacity to learn, this being exercised in the course of training for a part. The actor must be able to respond to fantasies and dreams, anxiety and excitement, resignation and apprehension.

The director then, is responsible for the action given to the actor. The phrase "all the world is a stage" is well known and, to the cinema actor, the world lies within a frame-line. He knows well that within that frame-line he can demonstrate the violent, the beautiful, the ugly, the sensuous, and all the vivid illusions of life.

ABOUT CRITICISM . . .

Criticism is a problem in obtaining objectivity. When the actor becomes negative in accepting criticism, he is allowing his personality to separate him from his work.

The director in criticising an actor should never be negative in his approach. He should supply a constructive substitute or suggestion. The suggestion should be clear and to the point.

A director should direct to relax the actor, be easy through the rehearsals and make use of the psychological moments to extend interpretations and emotions. The director should understand the actor to determine the type of individual with whom he is dealing. Does the actor respond to the rehearsals, then fall apart when a "take" is made? — or is the actor the kind of person who seems to relax in rehearsals, but comes through in the actual "take"?

The actor is not only a living character in the story, but the story is in the character. In the eyes of the audience, he must be given material which stimulates and establishes the significance of his character.

ESTABLISHING THE VISUAL IMPRESSION

Actions often speak louder than words . . . and similarly reactions often speak louder than actions. Staging should be logical, relaxed and motivated by the situation.

The study of the characterization should be thorough. The actor's energies should be directed into visual impression. Lines lacking motivation should be changed or deleted.

The director should work with the actor so that he delivers his lines, not only as a character speaks, but as the character thinks. He should aim at awakening particular background elements in an actor without prescribed form in which they must appear.

IMPORTANT OBJECTIVE . . .

The director must minimize tension for an actor. Tension is misplaced energy. When there is tension, one cannot think and feel properly and actions become forced. The actor must be given freedom to respond to his own objective thinking.

The actor must be led to "think" and "listen" to his role.

DIRECTOR AND TECHNICIAN RELATIONSHIP

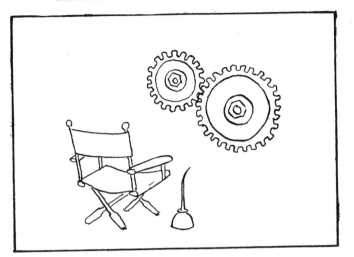

THE TECHNICIAN—THE MAIN WHEEL IN A PRODUCTION TEAM

The entire machinery of film production is a creative process which sometimes breaks down and exposes its separate parts.

The story analysis of individual background information, given by the director to the technician, causes scenes to play with well-oiled precision.

DRAMATIC EXPRESSION—PRE-PRODUCTION CONSIDERATIONS

The first considerations of production are the environment and backgrounds which surround the artists.

Interpretive mood and atmosphere must be determined by the art director before a production gets under way. Plans are drawn which are presented in the form of complete blueprints for the entire production. From these the play, from story to screen, materializes. In determining such plans, the following technical aspects must be considered:

How much does the director choose to shoot outside the studio using the natural settings dictated by the story?

What will be the considerations regarding sound, light, and construction problems in the various settings?

What will be the needs and systems of essential quality in lighting the interior sets?

INFORMATION THROUGH STORY ANALYSIS

A most important factor to be considered from director to technician is that all possible and meaningful information be used to define the theme and environment of the story. The entire production depends upon careful, detailed, artistic preparation of each scene in the film.

The right facts and information help the technician to create the environment he establishes for the total effect of the production.

ARTISTIC PROBLEMS—EXPRESSIVE CONTROL

The technique and mechanics of the design in a presentation depend upon the over-all production demands. The director must know where the focal points of the action will take place and precisely what mood he wishes to achieve which will be reflected in the design and construction of his sets. (The placement of doors, hallways, windows, sources for light, the background, the foreground elements, etc.).

The director works out the design of the story with the art director, who, in turn, finds "the way" through the director's composition. The art director keys all movements taken by mechanics, the camera, the sound, the lights, exits, entrances and the props.

The technician must understand the director's interpretation. He must know where and how the director will move his camera. He must consider the "fourth wall," reverse angles, establishing elements, developing shots, protection shots and any special effects the director has in mind.

Therefore, before the scenic artist begins to apply his own imagination to the problem of setting, he must confer with the director and the two must reach an understanding of the problems and intention.

The art director and the director of photography will confer with each other to further understand and resolve the problems. To achieve the esthetic effect there must be expressive control and a combined effort by the interpreters of the drama.

ENVIRONMENT IS THE CHIEF CONCERN

The art director is concerned about the character's "living background" and the element of visual environment. He must devise his sets for the action—interiors and exteriors. The settings he makes must place the action of the scene and also provide architectural and mechanical means for it. The components of definition such as light, shadow and all visual details must have a source and meaning. This source must be obvious to the audience.

The art director's contribution in utilizing sound and picture is largely measured by his instinctive use of dramatic, symbolic and conventional material.

EYE-TO-EYE PLANS—PRODUCER, DIRECTOR, ART DIRECTOR

Much of the information the art director needs must be extracted from the script.

The director and producer, with the art director, must see eye-to-eye before the final plans for dramatic presentation can materialize.

The art director, in the process of developing the field of action for the director, must check and re-check the properties, light sources, transitions, exits and entrances regarding camera and microphone maneuvering—all the essential requirements in the environmental static and moving composition.

The areas used by the director are measured by the art director. Both of these artists are highly interpretive—the final effect of both artists is unity of production.

The art director must have a comprehensive understanding of the limitations of "the field of action," the studio and location space. He must learn to compensate and control the use of the equipment necessary to work within such limitations. Such understanding will enable the director to give proper motivation to his actors and enable him to move his camera and microphone in a way that does not intrude upon the action being filmed.

The art director, then, works closely with the film director. The artistic judgment of both must be exercised with full consideration of existing limitations. Then, and only then, can the dramatic event become effective.

EFFECTIVE PRESENTATION . . .

The effectiveness of any production depends upon careful technical organization as well as creative imagination of the art director.

The purpose of scenery in an audio-visual medium is definite. Sets provide or suggest a suitable background for action and their quality and artistic value are measured solely by their appropriateness.

Scenery is interpretative. If a musical revue is gay and zany, the setting must be gay and zany. If a Shakespearian tragedy is somber, so is the setting. The setting must always complement the production.

Scenic design, like all creative functions, is not easily codified. There are different ways of staging a production in any given field where the action is to be presented. One method cannot be said to be superior to another, provided the final effect is one of unity.

The script content determines the path the designer follows in developing basic settings and it is mandatory that he become thoroughly conversant with the director's interpretation and intent. Much of the information the designer needs must be carefully extracted from the script.

EFFECTIVENESS IN A LIMITED FRAME-LINE COMPOSITION

Creative illusion is an important aspect when filming within a limited space. Presentational qualities of both picture and sound are dependent upon the allowed, designed perspective, oftentimes too limited, or not made possible by the very nature of the setting.

Use of mutual or source lighting to fit the mood and atmosphere of the scene is also vital in creating illusion. Following are a few simple illustrations suggesting the capability of an angle in the design to express a mood and perspective which allow freedom for camera and microphone to work within a limited frame-line composition.

The illustrations are made up of "stock" elements which need a minimum of construction.

LIGHT CAN BE CREATIVE . . .

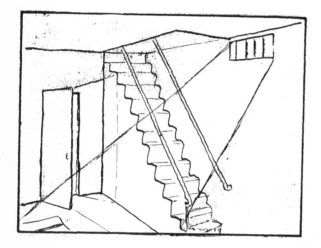
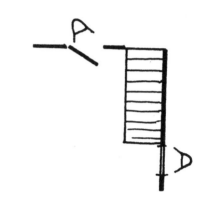

(figure 1) Light and Shadow help tell the story.

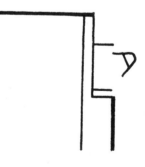

(figure 2) Mood lighting appeal to emotion.

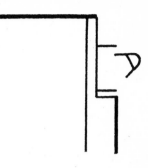

(figure 3) High brightness tends to
distract the attention from the
portions of interest upon which the
eye should be focused.

PERSPECTIVE CREATES . . .

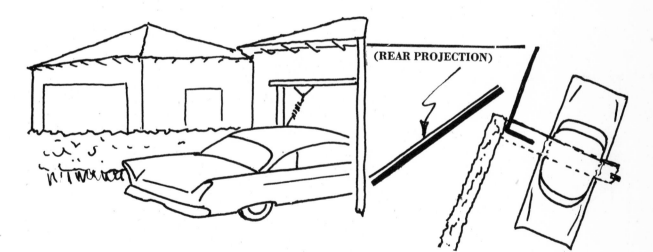

(REAR PROJECTION)

(figure 4) Automobile mock-up,
rear projection and basic set
combined to create realism.

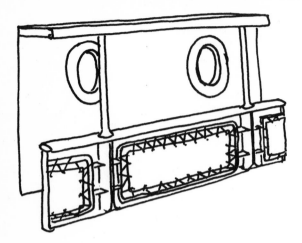
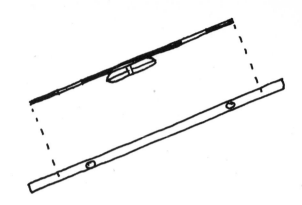

**(figure 5) The shipboard scene
created with a basic flat, a railing
piece and two stanchions.**

The art director and film director can visualize these settings to be properly designed so as to render the illusion needed.

A cyclorama background provides the perspective for the foreground elements.

THE STYLE OF THE ARTIST CREATES . . .

There are essentially three types of intimate scenic designs for limited frame-line filming.

(a) General utility backgrounds which serve as neutral backgrounds and denote no particular place or locale.

(b) Representational settings that do suggest or imply the realistic.

(c) Abstractions or stylizations which project or express dramatic meaning.

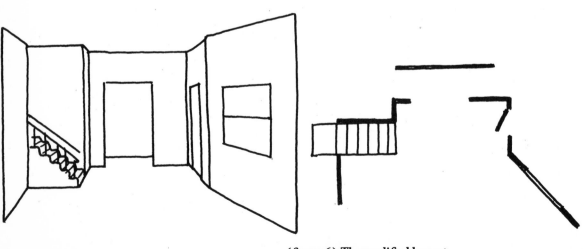

**(figure 6) The modified box set.
The right wall is angled to allow
greater freedom of camera and
microphone.**

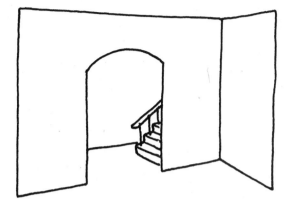

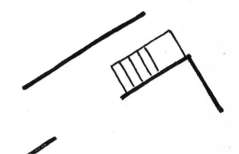

(figure 7) The setting is representational and proportionate to the action.

DESIGNER'S STYLE . . .

STYLE is an all-production element and demands consistency in all production phases. The designer's technique is as tangible as the tools and facilities he uses. Therefore, an artist dealing with the preparation of a realistic scene applies his own sense of design and creativeness in bringing out certain details.

Styles in scenic design are as diversified and confusing as Hamlet's catalogue of dramas chiefly because in a tri-dimensional medium involving actors and transitions, the designers must compromise on hyphenated-types rather than adapt pure styling methods easily employed by easel artist or sculptor.

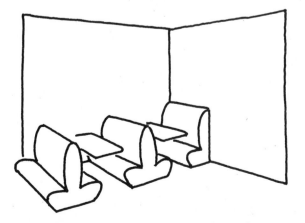

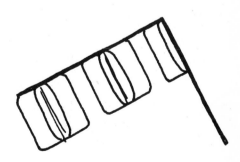

(figure 8) Simplicity is often the solution to the problem.

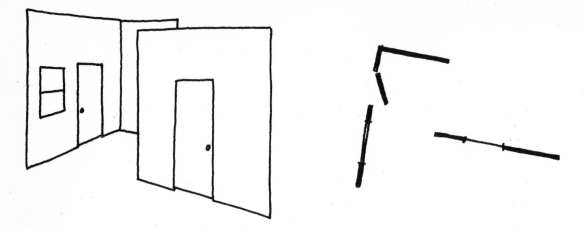

(figure 9) A design must provide
freedom for interpretation through
blocking cameras, microphones,
lights and actors.

Scenic elements themselves also include items which provide the stationary visual content of the program, exclusive of furniture, props, lighting, special effects or talent.

For motion pictures, an entire room might be set up for camera and microphone to range through the entire set. Simple elements may include anything from canvas covered flats to an elaborately constructed spiral staircase or other items from a three-foot platform to a fifty-foot painted drop of a row of tenements.

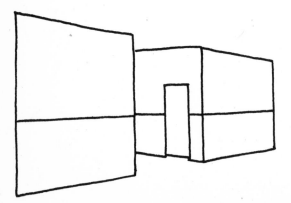

(figure 10) The set is designed for
reverse considerations. It is one-
dimensional.

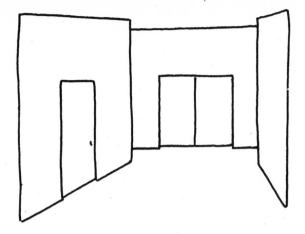

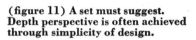

(figure 11) A set must suggest.
Depth perspective is often achieved
through simplicity of design.

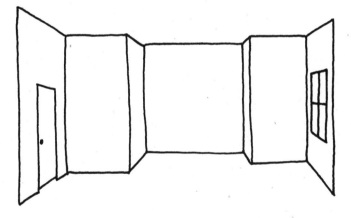

(figure 12) A set must have
character, mood and atmosphere.

CONSIDERATION OF THE AUDIENCE

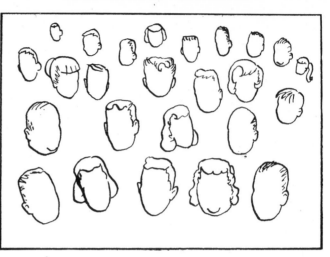

THE AUDIENCE—A WALL OF FACES WITH MIXED EMOTIONS

To know an audience is akin to seeing, hearing and reacting. It is to be alone on a wind swept hill or buried in the bowels of a coal mine. It is a feeling—an understanding. It is hating or loving, liking or disliking. It is a psychological process of life.

The director must strive to organize and present his material logically and build visually and vividly for the audience. He must work to affect the audience through different impressions. He must appeal to their ears, eyes, sense of motion and their reactions to the reasons and meanings which motivate their emotions. The director should control the drama through realistic motivation and cinematic techniques.

Many dramas adapted for the screen are dull and completely fail to entertain and keep interest alive. Why? Because the playwright or author, in his writing, has never stopped talking. When this happens, there is nothing left for the audience to do but to sit back, look and just listen, whether or not they like it.

THE AUDIENCE WANTS . . .

The audience wants to know what the show is all about. It wants to enjoy the superior position of knowing something about the story that the characters don't know. It likes to sit in judgment and enjoy the basic situations of the drama or comedy. It likes to sit in judgment of the hero or the villain. An audience likes to draw its own conclusions.

A "character-story" takes on dramatic interest when the audience finds out, or thinks it is finding out, something about the character that the character doesn't know about himself. The story usually ends when the character finds out what the audience has known all along, the inevitability of the character's destiny.

The straight story or tragedy, where the character is a victim of circumstances over which he has no control, is heightened dramatically when the audience discovers what the characters don't know.

The audience wants more than words. It wants to hear words of action that produce reaction. It wants to discover the theme, whether the story begins with a character or with a situation.

The audience looks for attitudes in a character, the way he eats, sleeps, walks; his every mannerism is as essential to the story, as seeing the story itself. The audience looks for character identification, wants to be drawn into the characters as well as into the plot. It seeks knowledge. It seeks contact and esthetic pleasure. It reacts in synchronization with the story, to sounds, meanings and motion.

THE AUDIENCE FINDS . . .

The spectator tends to identify himself with the character and situation, the misunderstood wife in the story, the conquering hero . . . and any experience which is emotionally gratifying and challenging. The audience should discover the artist.

The reactions by the audience constitute the emotional principle of identification of the character. The audience participates. It looks at something at which it can direct its emotions thus making it a part of the story. It joins emotionally as if it were actually there.

The audience is the ultimate challenge—its reactions are the only meaningful judgment of the finished product.

THE AUDIENCE REACTS . . .

There are no written laws or rules by which an artist can govern his interpretation. The "laws" of a craft are found in self-control nad in audience judgment. When they are broken, the artist fails.

The interpretive artist must have a clear understanding of what to look for. He must know what is wanted, how to get it and be able to recognize it when it is there.

The true artist has the capability and power to give meaning to inanimate objects through illusion. He can communicate his philosophy for consumption and consideration. He is geared for effects, tastes, devices and must possess an exquisite sense for detail. The detail in a composition is a balance to the total framework and the total image, be they true or illusionary.

The dedicated artist who first seeks truth can give realism a poetic clarity without blurring its naturalism. The first-rate artist, who strives for perfection through his keen perception, learns early to carefully weigh his judgment with responsibility before turning it loose on an audience. He must be aware of the governing powers of the unwritten "laws" that he will be facing. Upon understanding this, he is forced to create esthetically as he projects life, beauty and importance to an audience.

The story is the principal means by which the artist creates. The story is quintessential. Without story or theme, the artist cannot exist, the director cannot interpret, the actor cannot perform and the technician cannot design an esthetic impression which expresses his artistic endeavors. Story, in motion pictures, is communication through the sensitive expression of art and is designed to entertain and stimulate an audience.

Sensitivity in a projected theme is felt by the audience. The thematic perspective given to the images, which establishes a sense of reality, creates or destroys an awareness of the composition of an idea.

The visual, audible and emotional aspects can be placed in a composition so that the audience will react as a group and also as individuals. The composition can elicit an immediate response from the audience. It can make a lasting impression to be thought about as an experience and be evaluated by the individual.

In cinematic structure, illusion and reality are married to express a theme and emotional action. The focal point for an audience is inherent in every frame, unit of action, emotion and reaction of the film.

A DIRECTOR, AN ACTRESS, A CAMERAMAN, AND A SCHOLAR . . . When asked about audience, said:

"There are perhaps two kinds of pictures. The first begins with a very complicated story which has to be flattened out so that it is understandable to the audience. The second is a simple story with ornamentation. The second is my preference. I want the story to have the same appeal in Minneapolis as in Dusseldorf." BILLY WILDER, director.

"More important is to win for my films the attention and support of a world audience. I am, after all, an old hand at prize-winning. The time has now come not to work for awards, but to make pictures which will bring them back in." INGRID BERGMAN, actress.

"I believe that the audience should not become aware of contrivance, since this destroys the illusion. I try to reveal the picture through the lens subtly, but simply, without camera tricks. I am, too, aware not to waste the value in the right angle; the relationship to story demands; the director's desire; and finally, what the audience will expect to see on the screen. I concentrate my camera upon the character and the environment, and think of the camera only as a means of the audience getting close and living in the scene." STANLEY CORTEZ, cameraman.

"The playwright writes for an audience. He writes to affect it. The theater is a place where the spectattr can feast his senses. The theater is a place where the spectator can feast his senses. The for diversion, stimulation, and illusion, may be added also, sensation." SAMUEL SELDEN, scholar.

✿   ✿   ✿

Chapter 12

TELEVISION . . . LIVE

. . . Studio and Control Room Personnel . . . The Plight of the TV Director —The Technical Aspects Governing Him . . . Transitional Process of Editing Composition . . . Relationships of the TV Director to — STORY — WRITER — ACTOR . . . The Production Team . . . The Camera depends upon the Human Touch . . . The Terms the Television Director Uses . . . Informative Terms and Production Information for the TV Director and TV Producer . . .

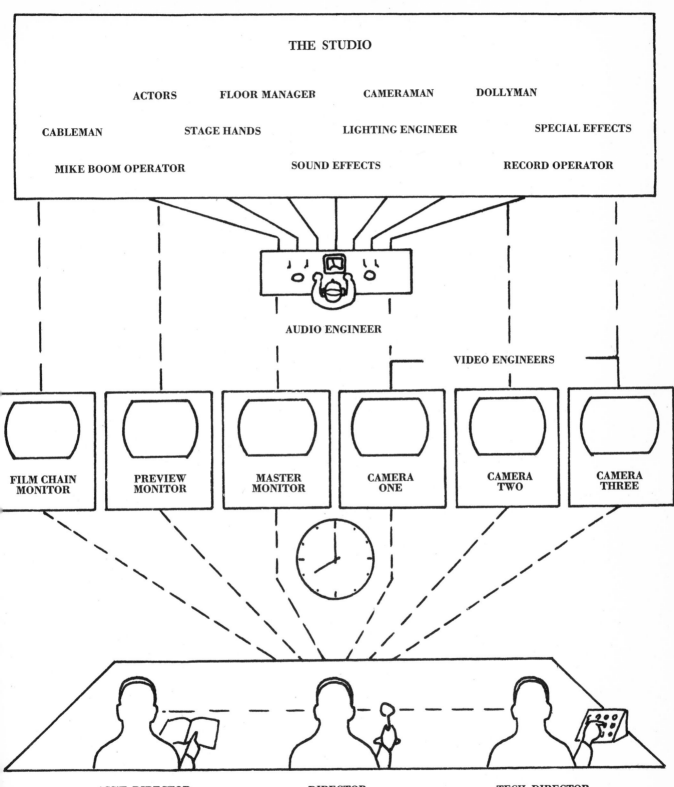

The illustration here shows single concept operation with fixed lighting and microphone positions pre-set for the actor. The studio space is limited and small, the movements confined.

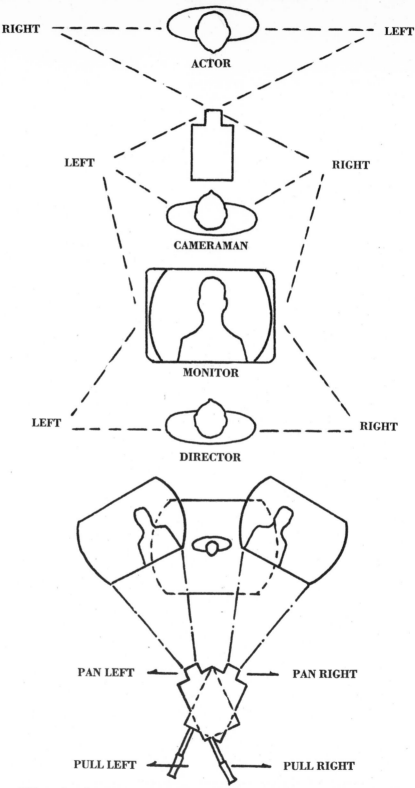

What the director sees on the camera monitor is the same as the cameraman sees in his viewfinder as he faces the actors. Therefore, the director's right and left are the same as camera right and camera left. The actor facing the camera must remember that "camera right" is his left, and "camera left" is his right.

Technology will undoubtedly develop new devices, improved media, and new techniques of production for the audio-visual media. Theatre, television, films may all change.

Nevertheless, the basic principles of live audio-visual presentation will remain and afford valuable insights to the creative originators and interpreters. Therefore, the following definition and the considerations for directing live television are presented.

THE PLIGHT OF THE TV DIRECTOR—THE TECHNICAL ASPECTS GOVERNING HIM . . .

In many aspects, the director in live television is no different from any other dramatic director. He must still be concerned with interpretation, emphasis, composition and the many other problems confronting a motion picture director or a stage director. However, he is apart from his colleagues in that he must project his story interpretations through electronic transmission. But this is not the principal governing factor of the TV director, which is TIME.

His program must begin and end at a prescribed time.

"TIME"—LIVE TELEVISION AND DIRECTOR

The structure of commercial television in the United States has been so established that time governs every aspect of its broadcasting hours. A sixty-minute show is not sixty minutes; it may be fifty-six or even fifty-two minutes because TIME must be alloted for the commercial message.

Television has become a means by which a company can obtain an audience, and this audience, in turn, becomes the buyers of the company's products. Television is a consumer's market. Theoretically, the greater number of people who see a commercial message, the greater the response in terms of increased sales and good will.

From the sponsor's point of view, television serves primarily for selling, with secondary emphasis on entertainment. To the director, television is primarily entertainment, with secondary emphasis on selling, yet the director of live television is forced to place equal emphasis on both aspects.

The effectiveness of a telecast depends upon the director's careful analysis of the story and selection of the emphasis as well as his own creativity and imagination.

From the very conception of the show, the TV director "fights" the clock in making it work for him. He must make every situation in the story coincide with time measured in seconds.

Those before the camera must also work with the clock as they pace their actions. The responsibility of reflecting proper development in interpretation lies with the director, who alone must find the freedom to fulfill characterizations.

The live TV director must learn to coordinate the use of music, lighting, graphics, set design, sound, color elements, makeup and special effects. Most important, as in all media, he must know story and be able to project his interpretation to the actor.

The director in live television is a technical artist, a coordinator of basic arts and a scenic conductor.

TRANSITIONAL PROCESS OF EDITING COMPOSITION

The television director must also learn and apply the principles governing pictorial and sound composition. As with film, the pictorial composition deals with the arrangement of action within a frame.

Sound composition is concerned with the coordination of selected sound effects to create perspective in mood and atmosphere.

Live TV staging is similar to that of film, except there is more of a continuous and constant contact between the actors and technicians during actual telecast.

There may be times when the director wishes for a special effect to break the proscenium in a dramatic show, such as insertion of film, which can present scenes in far away places. However, it is desirable to maintain the same presentational quality in the film as in the live action so there is no marked difference in transmission.

The TV director should study the imaginative and effective use of his studio space and set design in order to achieve his point of view. The director is responsible for proper motivation of the cameras.

The effectiveness of his total effort depends upon pre-planning, coordination and cooperation from his production team.

The TV director must learn the limitations and capabilities of the TV camera. Because of the viewer's limited size of proscenium, television requires emphasis on clear story interpretation through dialogue and the close-shot rather than through long shots and broad action. He must decide what perspective and camera composition will best tell the story. He selects picture-building composition as he edits the story. The TV director can build a dramatic relationship for the audience only if he understands and controls his selection of camera shots which tell the drama without disturbing the story.

In television, the continuity is the scene-by-scene action as it is played in continuity on the set. The single units of action are automatically linked together as the play moves forward. By comparison, in the motion picture medium the director may break his story line into parts, the joining of the actions to follow later in the editing. The film editor has the advantage of building the story and cutting out imperfections.

In television the director is both director and editor and performs these two functions simultaneously. He therefore is subjected to a greater possibility of error in selection. He may become engrossed with the freedom offered by the "cutting facilities," which may result in poor shot selection and composition.

Under the guise of artistic endeavor he often attempts "special effects" which break the theme of the story and draw attention to themselves.

The director should execute visual control of the story in such a way that the audience is never conscious of the working cameras—only of the unfolding story as it plays.

The TV director should carefully consider and analyze each transition and change so that proper emphasis of emotional expression is given to the story.

The director must recognize motivations as well as visual changes in order to project a feeling of constant development. His shots should be selected to express the interpretation most vividly in a balanced focus of attention. This is further accomplished through careful planning and selection of details.

The TV director must be alert so that he properly cuts from one shot to another without disturbing emphasis and dialogue.

Selection is a magic word a TV director must know how to perform. A sensitivity to such selectivity is paramount, for it results from a spontaneous decision. He should never forget the audience for a moment, since they are the focal point of his selection. He should learn, in the progression of scenes, how to maintain character, environment, mood, space, pace and story elements during his allotted time.

The TV director finds the expression of his creativity limited because of the editorial technique involved as the story is telecast to an audience.

The TV director must learn such simultaneous duties as:

1. "Editing" the scenes from a battery of monitors.

2. "Editing" the sound and the effects from precision-timed recording devices while at the same time—

3. Concerning himself with the logistics of all personnel and equipment on the studio floor during the production.

Because of the complexity of television production, the director's responsibility is greater in this medium than in any other. The psychological and dramatic effects he desires to create depend upon the spontaneous coordination of all the members of his production team, while, at the same time, he must be master of television's technical aspects.

LIVE TELEVISION DEMANDS . . .

The medium of live television requires a technical proficiency in pictorial and auditory arts. The study of the technical demands and techniques peculiar to television must be understood by the actor.

Live television production demands the director's ability to make unwavering, "on the spot" decisions. At the same time, he must know the capability of the several cameras he will be using.

A live TV director is a story editor at the same time as he is calling his shots.

Live television production utilizes the props and the scenery of the theatre, the camera-eye and shot sequence of the film, and the broadcasting frame-work of radio. While it embraces the techniques of theatre, film and radio, it is unlike them. Television is a "close-up" medium, the small screen of a TV receiver is the viewer's proscenium arch.

It is unlike theatre in that its continuous action does not take place within the limits of the proscenium. It is unlike film because the television show is edited as it is presented. It is unlike radio because sound is used to complement the visual.

RELATIONSHIPS OF THE TV DIRECTOR TO— STORY-WRITER-ACTOR

As with film, the "heart" of a live television production begins with the story. The story as it appears on the TV screen is not confined to the proscenium arch of the stage. The audience is not limited to a "seat out front." The audience is on the stage in a specific relationship with the actors, involved in their emotions, carried forward with the story, as the words and actions are seen and heard.

Television writing means writing for a close-up medium. The emphasis on the story is gained primarily through dialogue and close-ups rather than through action within the scene. The settings are usually confined to the studio. The social and physical structure of the story becomes subject to censorship and sponsorship.

Scripting for the television medium places emphasis on unique characteristics and dialogue. The choice of words and thought in dialogue is of significance to the physical structure.

The director constantly depends upon orientation and details to achieve appropriate visual attentions and motion of idea.

There is a definite need for writer-director relationship, although such relationship seldom exists. A fully developed teleplay is as indispensable to the dramatist as a set of plans to an architect.

The story must be translated by the director to meet the technical demands. The television writer and his story should create a theater as close to reality as permissible.

The theater of reality exists only when the illusion becomes united into a distinguishable whole—the actor becomes less the actor and more the real person. The actor in live TV is the same as that in motion pictures.

LIGHTING . . .

Studio lighting in live television production is generally done with an evenly saturated pattern.

Lighting should be plotted on a scaled plan of the studio by the lighting director. He should consider the backgrounds for effect and illusion. He must consider the limited space in order to create the dimension and atmosphere that the director's interpretation requires.

Staging action in the setting used for live television is not only restricted in space but scope as well. Lighting for mood then becomes a problem for the director.

GRAPHICS . . .

Graphics in television are a form of visual effects and information. Graphics include everything from a poster, used on a title stand, to more extensive art work used in backgrounds or settings.

The most commonly used of all visual effects is the TITLE CARD. In television, as in motion pictures, it is necessary that a certain number of words be used to explain. A standard size card 11x14 inches is considered satisfactory.

Proper contrast and definition must be considered in both title lettering and the art work. The boldness of the letter must also be considered.

THE TECHNICAL PERSONNEL . . .

The director and the assistant director are responsible for the over-all content of the program.

The engineering crew works under a technical director.

The Video engineer controls picture quality.

The Audio engineer controls all sound and music.

THE PROGRAMMING CONSOLE . . .

The programming console, at which the director and his assistant sit, is equipped with a studio talk-back microphone as well as a microphone to talk to the floor manager and/or the camera crew. At the console, the technical director is equipped with an intercom and headphones, which enable him to talk to the crew. A camera switching unit is before him. He also controls the film chain. Before and during the telecast, all activity in the studio must function from the orders given at the console.

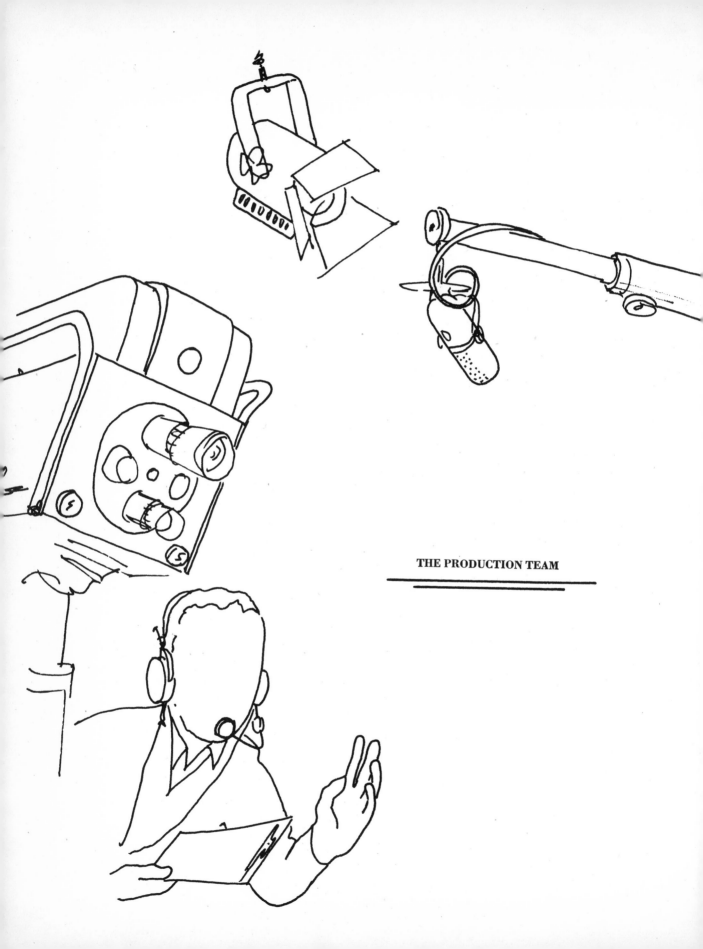

THE PRODUCTION TEAM

THE PRODUCTION TEAM

1. Programming Personnel

a. The Director

The programming side of this team consists of a DIRECTOR, assisted by an ASSISTANT DIRECTOR.

b. Assistant Director

The assistant director (AD) is a person who can perform many production tasks for the director. He follows the story and paces the action by the clock. He notes production set-ups as the director works out the action. He also watches the clock for the commercial breaks. He serves as a watchdog for TIME.

The assistant director takes over many of the details of production, leaving the director free to concentrate upon the story. He is the director's right hand.

He coordinates functions of the whole physical production and all its details including scenic elements, props, costumes, special effects, sound effects, make-up and scheduling of studio facilities.

2. Production Personnel

Television production, including technicians and artists, consists of a well-organized production team.

The production team must administer idea and story—casting and acting, design and scenery, costuming and make-up, studio and setting, sound and cameras and proper systems of lighting and directing. These are some of the important factors which determine the success or failure of a television production.

The understanding of special artistic techniques in the television medium is vital. Adaptability and originality must be evidenced and prepared for the viewer at all times.

a. The Audio Engineer

The audio engineer is completely responsible for the quality of sound which goes out over the air. Techniques in providing audio pick-up for TV more closely approach those of film-making than those of radio broadcasting.

b. Technical Director (TD)

The technical director (TD) is the executor of the director's wishes. He should be able to transmit directly to the engineers the director's ideas so that they may be put into immediate effect. His communication system is usually a telephone set and a small microphone.

c. Floor Manager

The Floor Manager is the director's "mouth-piece". He cues actors and arranges the sets and props. He manages the studio floor space during a production.

The effectiveness of a telecast depends not only upon careful organization but on full application of creative imagination, coupled with production team cooperation.

The production floor manager is, by the very nature of his title, a man of action who coordinates all movement on the stage during the telecast. He must be alert to all cues for actors, cameras and lights.

He is "logistics officer" of the telecast and is under direct command of the director. He has full control on the set.

d. Switcher (TD)

Switching (cutting from one camera picture to another) is performed by the technical director according to the director's instructions.

THE CAMERA DEPENDS UPON THE HUMAN TOUCH

TV CAMERAMEN are directly responsible for the operation of the cameras. Theirs is an important task, and they should be given as much leeway as possible in their artistic attempts to improve the quality of the show.

The TV cameraman should understand the limitations of TV composition. The director's creation will appear only through the technical skill and sensitivity of the team of cameramen which can anticipate the visual composition the director requires and do it.

The cameraman should remember that the camera is the apparatus which acts as a liaison between the director and the audience. Staging for the camera is a means of blocking the scenes by the director. The director blocks his actors so they relate to each other. His cameras are then blocked so they relate to the actor. The cameras are also blocked for the microphones.

THE TERMS USED BY A TELEVISION DIRECTOR

ABOVE:	An actor's cross behind another actor or stage prop. A crossing upstage or above.
AD-LIB:	To depart from the script or to proceed without script.
AREA:	"Playing space" or that part of the set.
ASIDE:	A line thrown away, not emphasized.
AUDIO:	Pertaining to sound portion of transmission; includes equipment such as microphones, amplifiers, cables.
BACKGROUND: (B.G.)	Any material, set, drape, drop, legs, hangings, rear screen, prop, section, etc., used behind actors or other foreground subjects.

BALANCE:	The audio relationships of voice, sound, and music; the blending of different kinds of sounds to achieve proper esthetic relationship.
B.G. MUSIC:	Background music. The music score for a program or film to heighten dramatic effect under dialogue.
BOOM:	Long metal arm for suspending a microphone which can be raised or lowered, extended or retracted.
BELOW:	An actor's cross in front of another.
B.G. SOUND:	Background sound. Exterior atmosphere, interior, exterior, street noises, outdoor effects.
BRIDGE:	A device for linking parts of a dramatic program; usually achieved through music.
BIX: (BUSINESS)	Action by actor pointing a line, stage action to complement dialogue. The exposition and staging.
CAMERA TERMS:	CU (close up). LS (long shot). MED (medium shot). XCU (extreme close shot). GROUP (a group of people or subjects).
CANNED MUSIC:	Transcribed or recorded music.
CLIMAX:	The pay-off.
CLOSED CIRCUIT:	Shows not actually broadcast, but transmitted to a limited number of sets.
CONTINUITY:	Progress from one scene to the next, maintaining character, naturalness, precision, space, pace and appropriate business.
CONTROL ROOM:	A small, sound-proofed, windowed room adjacent to the studio which contains the monitor panel.
COVER:	Blocking an actor or subject; blocking important detail from camera.
CROSS-FADE:	An over-lapping of sound, sound and music or voice. As one element is faded out, another is faded in over.
CRAWL:	Electronically or manually operated drum on which is placed a long strip of paper listing titles and credits. Drum revolves, bringing titles into frame.

CREDITS:	Cast list and job titles. Main and End.
CUE:	A signal to speaker, actor or a technician to start or perform an operation. Any individual line, scene or stage business which signals an off-stage actor to make his entrance. Signals from the floor manager.
CUSHION:	Music or talk used to fill in the time when a program runs short.
CUT:	In action, directing to stop a performance. In editing, to cut a scene, etc., to meet requirements. Immediate change from one picture to another. A breaking point.
CYCLORAMA:	A rounded backing or screen encircling the rear of the stage.
DIORAMA:	A miniature setting.
DISSOLVE:	The momentary overlapping of an image produced by one camera with that of another and the gradual elimination of the first image.
DOLLY:	A perambulator or four-wheeled platform. Camera or sound equipment to be mounted thereon.
DRESSING:	The set, objets d'art and hand props.
DRY REHEARSALS:	Without cameras or scenery.
FADE: (OUT or IN)	To decrease or increase volume gradually. To fade in or out the picture.
FLIP:	Art work on cardboard (often 9″ × 12″ but always in ratio of 4:3 designed to flip over on stand. (titles)
FM:	Frequency modulation.
FILTER:	An electric unit which controls the low or high frequencies—generally used to create the effect of a telephone conversation.
FOCUS:	Actor turns body and face toward another. Also to sharpen scene and detail.
FOREGROUND: (F.G.)	The area nearest the camera in use.
FOURTH WALL:	The imaginary wall completing a room. The wall which the camera displaces.

FRAME UP:	Instruction given to cameraman to center picture composition in camera viewfinder.
FREEZE ACTION:	Term used to indicate that the set design, arrangements, positions, furnishings, etc., to remain as they are. Action stops.
GAIN:	The amount of amplification.
GIVING THE SCENE:	Subordinate actor gives prominence to another actor.
HIT THE MUSIC:	Come in strong. Full volume at the opening of the music. On cue.
HAND PROPS:	Movable materials of all kinds used by actors.
HEAD ROOM:	The leeway between the actor's head and top of frame.
HIGH FIDELITY:	The accurate reproduction of musical tones.
KINESCOPE:	A film record obtained by photographing the tube picture directly with sound.
LAP DISSOLVE:	A superimposition fading gradually from one picture to another. A long dissolve.
LEVEL:	The amount of volume noted upon the meter of the control board.
LIBRETTO:	The book of a musical play.
LIVE TITLES:	Titling material which is photographed directly by television cameras in studio.
LOCALE:	The imaginary place where the scene is set.
LOOP:	A two-way circuit or line connecting the broadcast programs relayed for transmission.
MASTER CONTROL:	The central control room through which broadcast programs are relayed for transmission.
MONITOR:	To check action or review productions on a receiver. TV screen in control room.
MIX:	Combining the input of two or more microphones.
MIXER:	The panel of switches and dials by which program sound elements are blended and controlled.

MUSICAL BRIDGE:	A musical transition.
MUSICAL CURTAIN:	Musical or dramatic ending.
ON-MIKE:	To speak directly into the microphone at a proper distance.
ON THE NOSE:	A program which ends precisely on time.
ON THE AIR·	Program is in the process of being telecast.
MOTIVATION:	The reason which impels emotion, action or reaction.
MOOD:	Dominant emotional characteristic of the play, scene or set, atmosphere, time of day, season, locale.
FAX:	Facilities rehearsal—with camera.
MUSIC DOWN: or *UNDER:*	Music to be held behind speech or other sound, but not taken out entirely.
MUSIC UP:	Raise volume of music.
PAN:	To follow action to the right and left, with the camera. To pan left, or to pan right.
PERSPECTIVE:	Relationship of program sound elements from the standpoint of imaginative pictures created by the production.
REMOTE:	A program that is picked up from some point outside the studio. The show which originates outside television studio in a natural setting "on location".
RIDING GAIN:	Controlling the variations in volume.
RHYTHM:	The recurring emotional responses to the mood or objective of the script.
SEGUE:	A smooth and direct transition from one musical effect to another. Also applied to dramatic scene transitions and sound effects.
SCORING:	A musical background. Mood and tempo.
SNEAK IN:	To begin the sound effect or music very quietly and gradually increase the volume.
SNEAK OUT:	An imperceptibly slow fade-out in music or sound.
STAND BY:	Get ready, wait for cue. Command for alerting cast and crew.

SPLIT SCREEN: One-half of picture from one camera, and one-half of picture from another camera projected together on one screen.

STRETCH: Slow the tempo of your reading or music.

"TAKE":   Director's command to cut from one camera to another. Start the action.

TALK BACK: Phone circuit from director to his team.

TELEPROMPTER: Tape under magnifying glass attached to the top of camera containing the script or cues.

TEASER: Segment at opening of program before titles to interest the audience.

TEMPO: Variation of the pace or rhythm of script.

TILT: To follow the action up or down; tilt up or tilt down.

THEME MUSIC: Music which opens and closes a program, identifying music.

TRANSITION: Carry-across from one development—the scene, a sequence, a time, a place, a setting, a theme—to another. A transition may be effected by a music bridge, a fading out the speaker, by use of a sound effect or device and method as indicated by the director.

TRUCK: To move the camera in parallel motion with a moving figure.

TWIST: The unusual or unexpected.

VI: Volume indicator. Indicates the volume.

VIDEO CASSETTE: Film or video tape contained in a cartridge which can be inserted into projectors with a minimum or no threading of film or tape.

VIDEO TAPE: A stock for recording and production of program material.

INFORMATIVE TERMS AND PRODUCTION INFORMATION FOR THE TV DIRECTOR AND TV PRODUCER

ACROSS-THE-BOARD: Generally speaking it is an expression which refers to the entire sales campaign of a product; it is involved in the use of packaged programs, and commercials and any other method by which the product is exposed.

FILM LIBRARY: An actual library in which are categorized segments of film containing scenes and footages which may be used as inserts on various programs. The use of film for backgrounds and scene bridges serves many economical and production purposes.

Film may serve to identify a background, place or dramatic elements in a production with scenes of every description, such as:

Advertising; industrial; celebrities, past and present; events, current and historical; catastrophies and carnivals; fashions and floods; airplanes and animals; sports and science; scenic and civic shots from every part of the world.

Film footages (16mm) are stocked and indexed into small rolls, then inserted into slots in the library cabinet.

INSERT: Has virtually the same connotation in live television as the term has in film. It is a small scene or close-up of an object or objects which are "inserted" into the program continuity.

LIVE TAG: An announcement made live by a local announcer at the end of a filmed commercial message.

LENSES USED ON TV CAMERAS:

½ inch (12½mm)	WIDE ANGLE	60 degrees
1 inch (25mm)	WIDE ANGLE	30 degrees
2 inch (50mm)	CLOSE UP	15 degrees
3 inch (75mm)	FILM CHAIN	10 degrees
6 inch (150mm)	LONG LENS	5 degrees
ZOOMAR	Special Variable focal length.	

OPEN-END: That part of a commercial announcement that is left with a silent sound track to enable the use of a live tag. Sometimes a local card is used as the video image.

PACKAGE: A complete program idea, including the format and outline of the program. Oftentimes, the term refers to the complete program, ready for broadcasting, in a series of either 13, 26, or 39 "groups".

PRE-EMPTION: The superseding of one program by another —or one commercial by another.

PRIME TIME: "AA" and "A" time—which is determined by the number of sets in operation at a given time and are the peak viewing hours —usually between 7 and 10 p.m.

RESIDUE: Refers to all the material broadcast not having a direct affect on program content. Consists in part of all the film commercials, tags, credits and graphics.

SIGN-ON: The commencement of the program day.

SIGN-OFF: The end of the program day.

SPOTS: Purchased commercial messages.

TIME SALES: The process of securing revenue for a radio or television station through the process of selling "air time".

TV MARKET: Refers to the area of distribution and penetration of TV programming. Usually measured by the number of counties covered and the projection coverage of the entire country.

V.H.F.: *Very High Frequency.* Refers to the type of electronic transmission for "standard" television broadcasting stations.

U.H.F.: *Ultra High Frequency.* Refers to that type of electronic transmission. A certain number of UHF frequencies have been reserved by the Federal Communications Commission for educational purposes.

✤   ✤   ✤

Part II

Chapter 13

THE AUDIO-VISUAL MEDIA

... TO JOHN DOE

THE AUDIO-VISUAL MEDIA

A NOTE TO JOHN DOE . . .

If you wish to communicate your creative intention to an audience in an audio-visual presentation, whether you be professional or amateur, you must understand professional film-maker's standards. In this book we have articulated the basic considerations of the creative originator and interpreter.

You, John Doe, will find ample opportunity to consider the elements of film making within your own frame of reference. You will find the professional ideal a challenge which will continually develop your ability to originate and interpret ideas in the audio-visual media. In a swiftly moving world where communication through audio-visual media is not only possible but necessary, development of this ability becomes exciting and important.

As you explore the media, discover, and develop your capacity for a means of communication, you will be able to interpret your awareness of your environment, what you hear, what you think about yourself and others. You will draw inspiration from your discovery and will develop curiosity not only about subject matter, but also about techniques of production.

All YOU need to do is to have a start—

WHERE TO BEGIN?—Have an IDEA . . .

One way to begin is to formulate an IDEA.

An idea is the product of thought. The idea may inspire a scheme, a plan, a method, the gist of a specified action or situation.

The idea may be of something significant—a conception, a fancy, a mental image of some kind, a theme or motif. The idea might incite some provocative action.

An idea may be stimulated by another culture—its artwork or music. An idea may be inspired by a conversation, a poem or a song. The character of silence may even inspire an idea.

You may create a film from an idea intended to inform, entertain, inspire, provoke thought. It may become a comedy, tragedy, documentary, news report, commercial or an instructional presentation. It can be interpreted on any audio-visual media that is practicable for you.

An idea is as big as your imagination.

INCENTIVE . . .

Do something to express yourself. Put it on paper, draw it on a story-board format so you can look at it closely and study it carefully.

Can you visualize a scene-by-scene presentation? You can? What about the setting and environment? Are there principal characters involved? Do they have something to say? Do you know anything about these characters? Can you express what they think, how they think, where they live? How they live? Do you have a theme? Is there a plot?

Do you have a point of view to express picturization? Is sound composition to be narrative, to have background effect, dialogue and synchronization?

What medium—film; (35mm, 16mm, 8mm), filmstrip, cassette, TV, cinema?

How long will it be? Can it all be expressed in the audio-visual media?

PREPARATION . . .

The audio-visual media are a technical means for communicating ideas. You must understand the technology, techniques, capabilities and limitations of the media before you can use them effectively and creatively. Reading, alone, will not make you an instant film maker, nor will "experience", without reading or theory, make a film.

A student once decided to make a ten-minute film. The idea for the film was great, but the student knew nothing of the capabilities and limitations of the medium, had no previous experience, not even with a still camera. Though advised to make some preparation by reading and learning about the camera capability and limitation, requirements for film editing, lighting, staging and sound, the student plunged in without preparatory study.

The resultant movie had distracting camera movement, jerky visual continuity, unsynchronized sound, over and under-exposures, uninteresting camera angles and very few creative visual compositions. The student may have made mistakes on this first film, in any case, but had preparatory study been carried out and thoughtful planning undertaken, an excellent idea might have been more faithfully communicated to the audience.

More importantly, the student would have had a greater sense of reward and a greater personal incentive for the next production. Unless you are a quitter, there is always the next production to look forward to do.

You must combine study of theory, experience and experimentation if you want to develop your ability to communicate through the audio-visual media. You may not become a specialist in each technical job required in filmmaking, but your goal should be to learn enough to spot competency and creativity in the specialist and to use his skill properly in production of a film.

You must know your medium to use it creatively.

❉   ❉   ❉

Chapter 14

SET THE STAGE—FOR ACTION!

THE PRODUCTION PERSONNEL
of
"JOHN DOE'S"

SET THE STAGE—FOR ACTION!

NOTE TO JOHN DOE . . .

It is impossible to deal with *all* the conditions that may be encountered in an activity as varied and complex as film production. It is possible, however, to identify the most common production problems which you, John Doe, will meet within your frame of reference.

Let us describe the important duties for each crew member common to most productions. A crew member may be called upon to perform many duties outside his craft in his area of responsibility.

DIRECTOR—What does he do?

The director determines the content of the film. He is the prime creative force behind the production, giving it impetus and direction. He has ultimate responsibility for all aspects of the production. In addition to his creative functions during the shooting, he:

1. prepares the script for production, whether he is the interpreter or the original author;
2. selects the cast;
3. rehearses the cast and otherwise prepares it for the production;
4. makes his wishes known regarding the set, props, costumes, lighting, etc.;
5. selects locations;
6. assists the unit manager in planning the production budget and production schedule;
7. helps the assistant director plan the daily shooting schedules;
8. supervises a rough cut of the film.

The director is not concerned solely with directing the actors and selecting camera angles. He cannot stride onto the set on the first day of shooting, and find that the set has been designed and built, the lighting set up, the props and costumes assembled, the crew organized —all exactly as he intended them. All of these areas contribute to the success of the production, and all, therefore, are of immediate concern to the director.

The director must accept responsibility for making basic decisions in all areas of production, particularly as they affect the creative conception of the film.

He must make his wishes known to the other members of the crew, clearly and concretely, so they may carry out their work. He must follow up constantly to make sure his instructions are being carried out to his satisfaction.

However, the director's primary creative functions demand far too much of his time and energy to permit any detailed supervision of the other crew members. Having told them what he wishes to accomplish, he must rely on them to carry out their specific responsibilities.

ASSISTANT DIRECTOR

The assistant director's duties fall into two broad functions, he assists the director with all aspects of the director's work and supervises the crew during shooting. He does everything he can to facilitate the director's work, attempting to anticipate his needs and assuming as many of the incidental tasks as he can without lessening the director's control of the production.

He keeps in close touch with the director's activities, observing the casting, attending the rehearsals and following the progress of the script. He should be as thoroughly familiar with the creative aspects of the film as the director himself.

As head of crew during shooting, the assistant director is responsible for the conduct of the crew on the set. Working through the heads of the sub-crews, he supervises and coordinates the work of all crew members. He aims to run a smooth-running, efficient production operation.

His specific duties are to:

PRE-PRODUCTION PHASE

1. assist the director in conducting casting sessions;
2. assist the unit manager in conducting rehearsals;
3. assist the unit manager in preparing the production schedule;
4. conduct crew meetings;
5. assist the director with location scouting;
6. arrange for crew members to work on set construction, if necessary;
7. insure that crew members are adequately prepared for their jobs;

PRODUCTION PHASE

1. prepare and post the daily shooting schedule;
2. keep a directory of cast and crew members, indicating their addresses and telephone numbers;
3. supervise the positioning of equipment for each setup;
4. coordinate technical operation during takes;
5. keep the production on schedule;
6. direct the proper care and handling of equipment;
7. insure the proper maintenance and security of facilities;

POST PRODUCTION PHASE

1. supervise the striking of sets, props, and lighting equipment;
2. insure that the sound stage is left clean, lights are returned to their proper storage areas, props are returned, and location areas are restored to their original condition;
3. see that equipment is operable at all times.

UNIT MANAGER

The unit manager is the production's business and purchasing agent. His busiest time is the pre-production period, when he makes all necessary preparations for the production, with the exception of those having to do with the writing of the script, selection and preparation of the cast and the development of production designs.

Broadly speaking, he provides for all materials, equipment, facilities and services needed for the production. During the shooting period, he is concerned with those activities that take place off the set. (Operations on the set are, of course, the province of the assistant director.) He is not normally required to be present during the shooting. However, there may be occasions when his services are required.

Some of his specific duties are to:

PRE-PRODUCTION PHASE

1. prepare copies of the script and distribute them to cast and crew;
2. break down the script;
3. prepare the production budget for the producer;
4. draw up the production schedule;
5. submit requests for purchase orders to the producer and pick up items purchased and rented from the vendors;
6. maintain an account of expeditures;
7. arrange transportation for location trips;
8. arrange for hotel, meals, etc., for personnel and crew;
9. prepare a set cost form for each set with the assistance of the art director;
10. arrange for crew meetings;
11. arrange for photographic and sound tests;
12. arrange for editing facilities for the editor;

PRODUCTION PHASE

1. provide for the shipment of film to the lab and pickup of film from lab;
2. supervise the work load of the editor;
3. arrange for screening of rushes;
4. arrange for coding of the film;
5. provide for the developing and printing of still photographs;

POST-PRODUCTION PHASE

1. return rented and borrowed items to their sources;
2. supervise the turn-in of equipment.

ART DIRECTOR

The art director is concerned with the visual aspects of the film. His biggest job is the design of the set, but he is also concerned with such other visual elements as the props, costumes, makeup, lighting, titles, staging, camera angles, composition, special effects and credits, etc.

Although he is not required to be present throughout the shooting, the art director must be available when his services are needed.

1. do any research necessary to determine the character of the set, props, and costumes;
2. design the set and prepare plans for the use of the construction crew;
3. construct a model of the set;
4. make layouts to locate set pieces, set dressings, and greens;
5. design costumes and props, when required;
6. design special effects, when required, and supervise their preparation;
7. execute continuity sketches and mood and atmosphere sketches, when considered desirable;
8. assist the director in the selection of locations and advice on the preparation of locations for shooting;
9. assist the unit manager in determining the requirements;
10. design graphic material necessary for the production;
11. provide the unit manager with the necessary information about the set and assist him in budgeting the cost of construction;
12. advise on the appearance of special makeup if requested to do so;
13. diagram camera movements if requested to do so;
14. follow the progress of set construction;
15. act as liaison between the production and the construction supervisor;
16. supervise the work of the assistant art director if one is assigned;
17. supervise the dressing of the set;

PRODUCTION

1. supervise set changes;
2. advise the director on such matters as camera angles, blocking, composition, and lighting if requested to do so;
3. assist the director of photography with special photographic effects if requested to do so.

DIRECTOR OF PHOTOGRAPHY (Cameraman)

The director of photography is responsible for the photography of the film. As head of the photographic crew, he supervises all operations that relate to photography—lighting, camera placements, and movement, exposure, photographic effects, determination, etc.

The director of photography should keep in mind that the director has ultimate responsibility for the conception of the photographic image. Although he is encouraged to contribute ideas, he must be careful not to infringe on the director's prerogatives.

Some specific duties are to:

PRE-PRODUCTION PHASE

1. consult with the director on the photographic treatment of the film;

2. advise the art director on the design of the set from the photographic standpoint;
3. inform the unit manager of the camera equipment required;
4. insure that the required camera, lighting and grip equipment are on hand and in working order;
5. insure that the members of the camera crew are adequately prepared for their jobs;
6. conduct photographic tests if considered necessary;
7. inform the unit manager of the film stock required and insure its proper storage.

PRODUCTION PHASE

1. supervise the lighting through the gaffer (chief lighting technician);
2. supervise the placement of the camera and selection of lenses;
3. supervise the execution of camera movements;
4. determine the exposure;
5. devise and execute special photographic effects;
6. insure proper care and maintenance of camera equipment;
7. insure that the camera report is properly kept;
8. insure that exposed film is properly packaged and labeled for shipment to the lab and that developing and printing instructions are correct;
9. advise the director on photographic problems.

CAMERA OPERATOR

The camera operator is concerned primarily with the camera itself— its preparation for the take and its operation during the take. He takes his instructions from the director of photography.

The operator must make certain he is thoroughly familiar with the operation of the camera equipment before production begins.

Some specific duties are to:

1. set up the camera;
2. insure that magazines are properly loaded;
3. tread up the camera;
4. position the camera;
5. insure that shutter, aperture, focus and parallax are properly set;
6. check the sync motor;
7. insure that the camera is functioning properly;
8. operate the camera during rehearsals and takes;
9. advise the director of the adequacy of each take from the camera standpoint;
10. clean the camera, lenses and magazines at the end of each day's shooting.

CAMERA ASSISTANTS

The first and second assistant cameramen assist the camera operator, who determines the division of duties.

If two cameras are used simultaneously, the first assistant operates the second camera.

Some specific duties are to:

1. assist in setting up the camera;
2. load and unload magazines;
3. assist in positioning the camera;
4. assist in determining and setting the focus;
5. set the aperture, under the direction of the camera operator;
6. follow focus on moving shots and during takes when asked to;
7. perform all follow focus during shots;
8. make the slate;
9. keep the camera report;
10. assist in cleaning the equipment;
11. assist in making tests for the lenses.

CAMERA GRIP

If assigned, the camera grip assists in operating the dolly and in setting up and transporting camera and equipment.

GAFFER

The gaffer is the chief electrician and head of the electrical crew. He is responsible for carrying out the lighting instructions of the director of photography. Before production begins, he must make sure that he is aware of the rigging and understands the operation of the electrical equipment and the nature of the circuiting on the sound stage.

His specific duties are to:

1. assist the director of photography in checking that the needed lighting equipment is on hand and in working order;
2. supervise the rigging of the lighting instruments, cable, dimmer board, practical light sources and other electrical equipment;
3. supervise the directing and modifying of the lights, according to the instructions of the director of photography;
4. insure the proper handling of the lights and other electrical equipment by the electricians, paying particular attention to the demands of safety;
5. supervise the placement of reflectors for exterior photography;
6. insure that lights are unplugged at the end of the day's shooting and that light cables are coiled when not in use;
7. supervise the striking and storage of lighting equipment at the end of the production;
8. give the assistant director a detailed list of lighting equipment that needs repair;
9. take stock of all light bulbs and make sure that replacements are on hand;
10. have inventory on hand of all equipment used in the production;
11. serve as chief electrical supervisor for all lighting needs.

BEST BOY

As the gaffer's assistant, the chief grip assistant and camera department assistant (slate person) prop assistant, the best boy performs any duties assigned to him by these departments.

Each department may have its own best boy. In the electrical department, often, on the sound stage, he directs lighting activities on the catwalks, while the gaffer remains on the floor in close touch with the director of photography.

The best boy may also be assigned to operate the dimmer board or to execute any special lighting effects during a take or operate the generators on location set-ups.

ELECTRICIANS

The electricians handle the lighting and other electrical equipment under the direction of the gaffer.

MIXER

The mixer, who is head of the sound crew, is responsible for the sound recording of the film. His duties are outlined in detail by the staff sound engineer, who works closely with the mixer and other members of the sound crew.

His more important duties are to:

1. advise the director and assistant director on sound matters;
2. set sound levels and equalization;
3. act as final authority on the positioning of the microphones;
4. monitor sound takes and advise the director of the quality of the recording;
5. insure that sound equipment is turned off and properly stored after the day's shooting;
6. keep records of every take. (sound reports)

RECORDIST

The recordist operates the recorder and performs various routine tasks. He works under the direction of the mixer.

His specific duties are to:

1. prepare the sound stock for recording;
2. place the recording, transmission, and power equipment into operation;
3. maintain the sound log;
4. label the sound stock for proper identification.

BOOM MAN

The boom man, under the direction of the mixer

1. positions the microphone, microphone boom and perambulator;
2. operates the microphone boom during rehearsals and takes.

CABLE MAN

If assigned, the cable man

1. connects and positions sound cables;
2. assists boom man in moving the perambulator (moving platform for camera or microphone boom);
3. performs any other duties assigned by the mixer.

SCRIPT SUPERVISOR

The script supervisor keeps notes and records production information during shooting for the assistance of the director and editor (see "production records").

The script supervisor's duties are to:

1. advise the unit manager in advance of production of the supplies he will need for his work;
2. keep script notes and a shot record;
3. make such other notes and a shot record as the director and assistant director may request;
4. advise the director on the completeness of the shot coverage;
5. have complete knowledge of the script and breakdown;
6. point out to the assistant director occasions when stills would be helpful for matching purposes;
7. insure that information on the slates is correct;
8. keep in possession a copy of the daily shooting schedule, if requested, and advise the assistant director of the progress of the day's shooting;
9. keep on hand a copy of the script for the reference of the director and other crew members;
10. keep on hand a copy of production notes for the producer;
11. obtain two copies of the camera report from the camera crew at the end of each day's shooting and submit one copy to the assistant director and the other to the editor at the end of the production;
12. make a copy of the annotated script and the shot record and submit them to the assistant director at the end of the production;
13. submit the original annotated script and the shot record to the editor at the end of the production;
14. perform such other clerical duties as the assistant director and unit manager request, such as preparing copies of the script and typing correspondence;
15. work directly in cooperation with the director at all times. A script supervisor is like a good girl Friday.

PROP SUPERVISOR

The prop supervisor is in charge of the props and set dressings during production.

His specific duties are to:

1. assist the unit manager in determining the requirements for props;
2. assist the unit manager in procuring props and set dressings;
3. advise the unit manager of any supplies needed for proper maintenance and storage of the props and set dressings;
4. act as set dresser under the supervision of the art director;
5. insure that props and set dressings are properly handled and safeguarded when they are in use;
6. insure that props and set dressings are properly stored when not in use;
7. perform minor repairs on props and set dressings when necessary;
8. assist the unit manager in returning the props and set dressings to their sources;
9. supervise the authentic special props that may be required.

WARDROBE SUPERVISOR

The wardrobe supervisor is in charge of the costumes during production.

His specific duties are to:

1. assist the unit manager in determining the requirements for costumes;
2. obtain information on the clothing sizes of cast members for whom costumes must be obtained;
3. assist the unit manager in procuring costumes;
4. advise the unit manager of any supplies required for the proper maintenance and storage of the costumes;
5. assist in the making of any wardrobe tests considered necessary;
6. store costumes when they are not in use;
7. assist cast members in putting on costumes;
8. make minor alterations on costumes when necessary;
9. advise the unit manager whether rented costumes should be laundered before they are returned;
10. assist the unit manager in returning the costumes to their sources.

MAKE-UP SUPERVISOR

The make-up supervisor applies make-up to the cast members during production.

His specific duties are to:

1. assist the unit manager in determining what make-up supplies are on hand and what additional supplies must be obtained;
2. assist the unit manager in procuring make-up;
3. assist with any make-up tests when required;
4. organize and maintain the make-up room on the sound stage;

5. apply make-up as necessary;
6. utilize special hair-pieces as necessary;
7. supervise the assistant make-up person if such person is assigned;
8. store make-up at the end of the production for use in succeeding productions.

STILL PHOTOGRAPHER

The still photographer, supervised by the assistant director, takes production stills and does any other still photography required.
His specific duties are to:

1. assist the unit manager in checking the still equipment to insure that it is on hand and in working order;
2. assist the unit manager in determining the requirements for still film and developing and printing services;
3. take all production stills as necessary;
4. take other stills that may be required, such as location stills and photographs required for special effects or as props, or as the producer will direct for publicity and advertising as the production warrants;
5. prepare exposed still film for shipment to the lab and insure that it is accompanied by the proper developing and printing instructions;
6. make "slop" tests if requested by the cameraman.

KEY GRIP

As the chief grip, the key grip supervises and participates in the work of the other grips. He takes his instructions from the assistant director.
His specific duties are to:

1. advise the unit manager of the hand tools that should be on hand during the production;
2. insure the proper use of tools and grip equipment;
3. insure that sound stage and location areas are left clean at the end of the day;
4. furnish the assistant director with a list of any tools that need replacement or repair. (studio operation)

GRIPS

The grips perform miscellaneous construction and provide general labor under the supervision of the key grip.
Specific duties are to:

1. make modifications in the set during production, such as removal and replacement of wild walls;

2. perform miscellaneous construction, such as the laying of dolly tracks, assembly of parallels and scaffolds, rigging for backgrounds, backdrops and lighting;

3. construct additional platforms as may be necessary to follow focus on the camera dolly;

4. assist in operating the camera dolly for moving shots;
5. assist the electrical crew in rigging lights if requested to do so;
6. assist the sound crew in rigging cable and moving the perambulator if requested to do so;
7. clean the sound stage or location area at the end of the shooting day;
8. assist in transporting equipment and supplies.

EDITOR

The film editor works under the management of the producer, usually on a contractual basis. He accomplishes the editing operations through the assembly stages until the "answer print" is in the producer's hands.

Usually the film editor maintains his own staff of assistants to accomplish the required work.

His specific duties are to:

1. advise the unit manager or producer of the facilities, equipment, and supplies required for the production;
2. "sync—the dailies"—synchronize the picture and sound track;
3. prepare the film for coding;
4. break down the film—all footages—and make an assembly of all the shots;
5. supervise all editing services as necessary until the "answer print" (first print from the lab) is approved;
6. keep storage space available and make a complete index of all exposed footages, unedited and edited scenes, including all takes, sound tracks, tapes and effects;
7. keep a complete and accurate record of all scenes including out-takes until the completion of editing;
8. maintain storage racks and empty film cans;
9. arrange all screenings of the "rushes", first cut and all subsequent cuts until the answer print;
10. prepare the picture and track, A & B rolls, supervise re-recording and mixing—arrange for matching the negative. Work closely with the laboratory. Order fine-grains and inter-positives to be used for optical effects—do all editing as well as supervising all the editing work by his assistants. He serves as the producer directs. Keep an accurate accounting and records for the laboratory orders that he has instigated. Serve not only creatively but as a business man as well. Run his craft as a business.

MANAGING THE CREW

Handling the crew is an exercise in leadership. Crew members are required to spend long hours at work that is sometimes difficult and demanding. Keeping up the morale and efficiency can be a challenge. The key and production chiefs are responsible for each of their members in their department.

It is beyond our scope to discuss the techniques of personnel management. Let us say only that those in positions of authority, particularly the director, the producer, and the assistant director, and even the unit manager, should give careful thought to how they can encourage the other crew members to do their best willingly and expeditiously. Furthermore, they should attempt to generate in the crew a degree of excitement and enthusiasm about the production that moves them to contribute far more than the minimal performance of the demands of the job.

CODING

Usually, time does not allow coding the film before the rushes, but coding should be done as early as possible, before the film is handled extensively. Obviously, the film cannot be broken down until after it is coded.

The film editor prepares the footage for coding, clearly marking the necessary instructions on the cans.

BREAKDOWN AND ASSEMBLY

After the film is coded, the editor breaks the footage down into separate shots and makes an assembly of all film footage and cross-indexes every shot, every scene, take and sound track.

The editor attends to all sound transfers, optical and sound printing. The original tapes are stored until the producer arranges for his own storage of the picture negatives and sound negatives.

Fine grains, interpositives, titles and art work on film will be stored by the producer.

SYNCING THE RUSHES

The work print is turned over to the editor when it is delivered from the lab. The work track (sound) is made by the sound engineer.

The method used to sync (synchronize) rushes has to do with the procedure employed for coding films. The coding has two purposes, to sync the work print and work track and to sync the work track and the original track. In order to accomplish both of these in the same coding operation, the work print, work track and original track must be in sync rolls of the same length. Since the original track is not cut into the picture until the very end of the editing process, the work print (which is always shorter than the sound) must be made to match the two uncut tracks.

The editor prepares the rushes by cutting apart each action shot, syncing it to the corresponding take in the work track and spacing the shots with leader so that the action roll matches the uncut work track.

Projection facilities must be arranged for "looking at the dailies"— looking at each day's shooting (rushes). This examination will indicate need for retakes, camera damage to the film, laboratory damage to film, over or under-exposed scenes, etc.

PRODUCTION NOTES

Of great importance are script notes and shot records. The script supervisor maintains a copy of the script on which are indicated any changes made in the action and in dialogue during shooting. Continuity details are important and must be exact in order to aid the film editor to do his work properly.

The script supervisor also lines the script to indicate the director's evaluation of the scenes.

At the end of the production, the script supervisor makes a copy of the annotated script and shot record and submits them to the assistant director for inclusion in the production record. The original script and record are turned over to the editor for use in his work. At the conclusion of the editor's work, the material all belongs to the producer.

CAMERA REPORTS

The camera reports are made in triplicate by one of the assistant cameramen. One copy is retained by the camera crew for future reference. The other two copies are turned over to the script supervisor at the end of each day's shooting. At the end of the production, the script supervisor submits one set of camera reports to the editor and the other set to the assistant director for inclusion in the production record for the producer.

SOUND LOG

The sound log is maintained by the mixer in triplicate. One copy is for the use of the editor and one is stored with the protection master (a master copy kept in the event anything happens to the original tape.)

STILL PHOTOGRAPHS

The most important single purpose of stills is to provide a graphic record of sets and set dressings, props, the costuming and make-up of the actors, basic lighting, setups, etc., should retakes be required at some future date. Throughout production the assistant director and still photographer must analyze the elements which should be covered.

Polaroid photographs can be useful during the shooting to assist the director with matching and continuity matters and to provide a quick on-the-set check on the effectiveness of lighting, make-up, special effects, blocking and composition, etc.

Photographs are also required for publicizing the film production and for general promotional work. What is needed, in this respect, are shots covering the high points in the action from the point of view of the motion picture camera and views of the cast and crew in action during rehearsals and takes.

Key personnel should be aware of the possibilities for using stills in other ways—in scouting locations and planning location shooting, in casting, in planning camera set-ups and staging during the rehearsal period. In planning the shooting, the director may even make a still for each shot, in lieu of continuity sketches, using substitute actors and makeshift sets if necessary. Stills are normally taken in black and white, although in the case of a production photographed in color, it may be desirable to make some production stills in color.

The asistant director includes a complete set of stills in the production record, eliminating only those that are not of adequate quality or those that are virtual duplicates. Negatives should be kept on file.

All photographs taken by the still photographer are the property of the producer.

Still photographers generally work on a contractual basis, whether for the duration of the job or by the day.

A SPECIAL NOTE TO JOHN DOE...

Programming and manufacture for the audio-visual media comprise one of the largest industries in the world. This includes the satellite industries that provide services and maintenance and develop merchandising of products as an outgrowth of the parent industry. They have explored communicating through audio-visual media and discovered their own particular speciality which they continue to pursue professionally.

You may not wish to become professional, but nevertheless wish to explore all types of creative and technical specialties that are necessary to create a presentation.

Not all of the personnel listed in this chapter will be needed for every production. The number of personnel will depend upon the type and complexity of the production. For simple productions, the job may be carried out by the originator—interpreter and one or two other persons. However, whether the job is simple or complex, a knowledge of the overall responsibilities is necessary for quality work and for growth and development of the originator-interpreter—you, John Doe.

Your services as a creative originator-interpreter will be useful in many fields not directly related to the industry.

To learn that you have the creative ability to work in the audio-visual media can become a most rewarding experience. It is for the John Doe, too, who makes home movies and tapes, who likes photography, who needs to define more carefully his CREATIVE INTENTION for a clearer interpretation of his subject or story.

You will have the opportunity to use the audio-visual media for such purposes as:

> Sales presentations
> Reporting
> Training
> Instructing
> Advertising
> Community Relations
> Documentaries

Demonstrations
Literary and Dramatic Presentations
Public Information

In such areas as:

Business and Industry
Education
Health and Welfare
Agriculture
Government (city, county, state, national)
Science
Religion
Recreation and Sports
Housing
Space Technology
Research and Experiment
Development Programs, etc.

*   *   *

Chapter 15

PUTTING THE VISUAL TOGETHER
Scripting...
Editing...
Composition...

PUTTING THE VISUAL TOGETHER

Films (35mm, 16mm, 8mm,) are made up of a series of moving pictures taken in different places at different times.

A film is generally produced from a detailed script. A slate bearing the name of the film, scene number, take number and sound number (if no sound, the word "silent") is photographed at the beginning of each scene. This information is necessary to the orderly filing and assembly of the film.

Sound is also recorded on the film and tape in exact frame-line synchronization with the picture. The recorder and the camera roll at the same sync speed.

Each shot is called a "take" or a scene. The joining together of these scenes, integrated and combined with sound, effects, music and transition, following the order of the scenario, becomes the basis for the process of editing.

Each scene is filmed from a position with a specified shot. There are three basic shots.

LONG SHOT: Allows a full view of the subject. The shot is considered an orientation shot and establishes the WHAT, WHERE, and the WHY of the scene. (see illustrations (a), p. 149 (k), p. **151** Part One)

MEDIUM SHOT: The subject emerges in a closer view than in the long shot. Only the necessary details are included. The medium view may be considered a developing shot. (see illustration (b), p. **149** Part One.)

CLOSE SHOT: A close view of a subject or object emerges into full and significant detail in the "close-up". The close view is meant to reveal an undisturbed meaning for the scene. The close-up is considered also an emotional value shot. (see illustrations (c), and (d), p. 149 (e), p. **150** Part One.)

For a better understanding and explanation of the basic and other shots refer to Chapter Ten, "Geography of a Camera Shot", p. 157, Part One.

There are no written laws to govern the making up of a sequence. In establishing a scene you may elect to start with a LONG SHOT. You may begin with a CLOSE SHOT.

(1) Long Shot

(2) Close Shot

Use mediums, (Two-shot, Three-shot, Group-shot) to develop and sustain interest. Change the point of view frequently as the content develops.

Use close-ups freely for emphasizing and expressing emotion and details.

Further variations and different angles along with a moving shot can be made of each scene and sequence. Move the camera only when there is reason and meaning. The basic shots or orientation—the master take, development shots and conclusive shots depend upon the type of subject and the interpretation.

THE ANGLE ...

Creative treatment counts heavily in the planning of your film story. Try for some imaginative camera angles. Each scene should have a reason and meaning for being there, and it should relate logically to the preceding and following scenes.

When composing a scene, shots can vary according to the angle from which they are taken. There are low-angle shots taken, looking upward, high-angle shots taken, looking down, on the subject. In some cases the camera may MOVE during a shot, either PANNING when it is swung horizontally, or TRACKING when it is moved along bodily. A shot may be a TILT-UP or TILT-DOWN with or upon a subject. The subject may move into a CAMERA'S CLOSE-UP or the CAMERA may PULL-BACK from a CLOSE-UP of the subject to a LONG-SHOT.

REVERSE ANGLE

A REVERSE ANGLE is the exact reversing of the point-of-view or angle of a scene. "The other wall." The shots taken in a reverse angle must match so that they are same at the point at which the shots join.

For example, a subject as he exits from inside a room should be at the very same point at which the succeeding shot joins.

If the subject's left foot is thrust forward as in illustration (3), the reverse angle shot should also show the same foot thrust forward as in illustration (4).

(3)

(4)

SCREEN DIRECTION

Note carefully the direction of movement. If you are following a character or subject with the camera from one place to another in a series of shots, you must not allow the character or subject to move across the screen from right to left in one shot and from left to right in the next.

If you do, the impression will be disturbing and appear that the action has suddenly turned around.

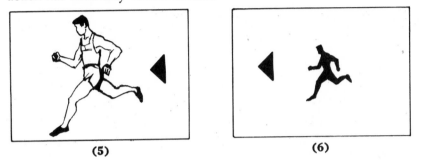

(5)   (6)

In reality, keep the flow of the action moving consistently from left to right or right to left, as the case may be.

The character should have the same expression in very nearly the same attitude at the point of joining.

If you are joining two shots of a fast moving object or subject, permit it to move appreciably farther in the first frame of the second shot and the result will appear natural. The joining of two shots together at a point where the characters are moving, is known as a "cut-in" in the action.

"MISPLACED" PERSPECTIVE

One of the easiest pitfalls into which the novice director falls is the misplaced camera perspective.

In the two illustrations below the characters seem to be going in opposite directions. However, they are the same character going in the same direction. The effect results from placing two cameras virtually opposite each other and shooting towards each other, while the same character walks between them.

(7)

(8)

Shots in which the subject moves out of the frame as in illustration (7), should be out *after* he has left the frame, not before, as in illustration (8).

(9)   (10)

Make the cut just a frame *before* the screen becomes completely empty. A shot must be exceptional and have an intrinsic interest to justify its being held too long. The shot may be held to lend suspense, surprise, shock, anticipate or foretell an event.

A general rule is to eliminate all portions of film in which nothing is happening which would otherwise slow down or stop the flow of the action.

Empty frames, that is, empty of characters or movement, must be cut out unless they serve a specific purpose.

EFFECTING SCENE PERSPECTIVE—Match the Action from Shot to Shot—

(11)   (12)

Through proper cutting, the audience is kept informed as to where the subject (illustration) (11) is going and where he has come from (illustration) (12). It results in a smooth transition from one scene to the next.

A cut to a shot appreciably nearer or further away has the effect of smoothly developing the point of view.

Never join two separate shots taken from the same view-point, but with the subjects in at least slightly different positions.

The master take (establishing shot) of a scene centered on a whole piece of action should be broken up into single points of view according to the meaning and development of the story. Establish the scene in the master take. Subsequent shots are breakdowns which differ in size, perspective and emphasis from the master.

(13)   (14)

In illustration (13), a character is established as looking at something through curtains. In illustration (14), the scene shows his **POV** (point of view), or what he is looking at.

VARIETY AND INSERT SCENES

Add variety and meaning to each angle. Pace your scenes until the climax is reached. A series of shots following quickly one upon another adds to the sense of excitement and enhances the effect of the dramatic sequence, particularly when close-ups and medium-close shots are used.

(15)   (16)

Going from a **TWO-SHOT** to a **CLOSE SHOT** provides variety, contrast, emphasis development.

"CUT-IN" and "CUT-AWAY" scenes (INSERTS) are bridges that develop, sustain and motivate the interest of story. The use of inserts, that is, cutting in a shot from a different angle or a close-up, can provide a brief time lapse. To serve its purpose properly, an insert must be relevant to the subject. Inserts, properly matched, keep the film moving.

CLOSE SHOT of one subject—to CLOSE SHOT of another subject.

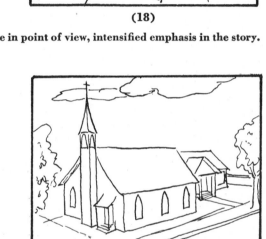

(17)   **(18)**

Provides change in point of view, intensified emphasis in the story.

ORIENTATION

(19)   **(20)**

If the church is the focal point for orientation, then the shot in illustration (19), becomes a "busy" shot. There is too much visual information. The shot in illustration (20), is then the proper shot.

(21)   **(22)**

The MASTER SHOT in illustration (21) establishes a character coming through the door. The next shot in illustration (22) shows his point of view (orientation), in this case, a reaction of the individuals on the couch to the intruder.

MOTIVATION

Motivation is impulse, incentive, reason, emotion which causes action. Some examples: MOTIVATED and UNMOTIVATED EDITING—

A MEDIUM SHOT of a subject, illustration (23), to a MEDIUM SHOT of the same subject, illustration (24).

(23)

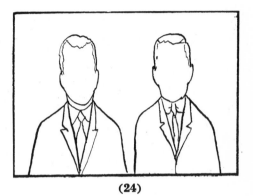

(24)

Provides no contrast, no variety, no emphasis, and delays the story development.

A CLOSE REVERSE SHOT of one subject to the TWO-SHOT, illustration (25), to a CLOSE REVERSE SHOT of the other person in this TWO-SHOT, illustration (26).

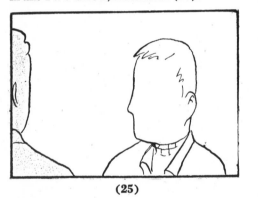

(25)

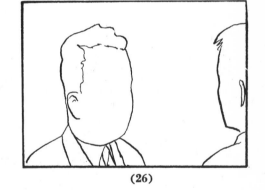

(26)

Provides contrast in reaction, variety and development in the emphasis of a story.

A CLOSE SHOT to a TIGHT SHOT in the GROUP provides contrast, variety in emphasis and story.

(27)

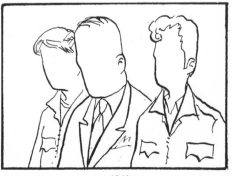

(28)

DURATION OF A SHOT

The time a shot should remain on the screen depends upon the time it takes for the audience to recognize its content. Titles or close-ups of reading matter should be held long enough to be read comfortably. A shot should only give a general impression of the scene.

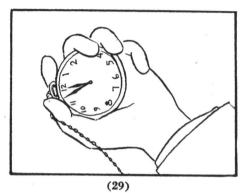

(29)

A simple subject such as a clock, letter, telephone, photo, etc., should remain on the screen only long enough for the detail to be read or understood.

A shot must be held long enough to recognize its content but no longer than is warranted by the interest it creates.

A shot, then, should be neither so brief that it cannot be properly identified, nor so long that the viewer becomes conscious of waiting for the next shot.

CHANGE

In the process of the pursuit of ideas, change is an important factor to help stimulate development of ideas. It promotes, develops and motivates different meanings and effects. It helps to express a theme.

Change in picturization makes possible a pattern of artistic impressions which expresses and heightens the dramatization. Change provides the basis for mood. In story structure, it constitutes TRANSITION from one value to another. In the cinematic technique, the different values in story form progress until the final climactic value is reached and accomplished.

CONTINUITY

A story is a thing becoming. Continuity of the format of a story is the process of calculated order and inter-relationship of parts. Continuity in story structure is a matter of weaving preceding and succeeding actions into dramatic union.

Continuity in film describes the smooth, logical, thematic connection from shot to shot. Picturization moves as a subject matter develops matching in every detail as it moves. It is effected by transition, arrangement and point of view.

TRANSITION

Action must advance from scene to scene until it is resolved. Transition is the "connector" or "bridge" from one scene to another. Without transition, a film story would advance in a jerky, episodic fashion.

Transition has been discussed in some detail in Chapter Eight, Part One. Here we are concerned specifically with one of the three means of transition, the mechanical.

Consider the methods of mechanical transition—fade, superimposition, dissolve, cut, and optical effects (there are approximately 150 different effects).

FADE:	is the process of gradually bringing a picture into being—or the taking the picture out from view.
FADE-IN:	an effect that starts with total darkness on the screen and gradually reaches normal picture density.
FADE-OUT:	an effect that starts with a normal picture density on the screen and gradually reaches total darkness.
SUPERIMPOSE:	is a fade-in of one scene superimposed upon pictures or images over the other. The effect is that of a double exposure in photography.
DISSOLVE:	is a fade-in of one scene superimposed upon a fade-out of another scene.
CUT:	is a break in the visual action by a direct change—a scene and or action change to another scene and or action.
OPTICAL EFFECTS:	are aligned on the film through a process of matte photography, frame by frame, within the effect until its finish.

Fade-in usually begins the scene or story. Fades and dissolves are useful for rounding off sequences and separating one subject from another.

A fade-out has a certain finality about it and gives a smooth conclusion to a scene or story.

A fade-out followed by a fade-in may suggest a time lapse, whereas a straight cut, from one shot to the next, suggests an abrupt jump in the story and action.

A dissolve from one scene to another suggests a shorter time than the fade-out and fade-in combination. It can also suggest a change of place or character.

A superimposure creates an illusion such as a dream sequence, a montage of events or impressions, a sense of confusion, or a flash-back in time, place, memory or events.

The cut from one frame to another eliminates the reality of action which is not necessary to an audience's understanding of what has taken place. For instance, a man is seen in a car driving along a highway. The camera does not have to follow the man for the fifty miles of his journey to convey to an audience that he is traveling fifty miles.

The cut, from his driving on the highway to his slowing down for a traffic light at a busy intersection, tells the audience that he has traveled and is near his destination in a town or city.

When visual material is "cut-in" or inserted, the effect is to "stretch" the action.

A "cut-away" condenses the action or time and provides different emphasis or development.

MATCHING THE ACTION

When editing the film, the editor depends upon the action at the beginning of every new scene to match perfectly in every detail with the preceding scene.

Consequently, the director must "overlap" the action at the end of every preceding scene to the very next succeeding scene.

This is called "dove-tailing" the action of the succeeding scene with the preceding scene.

The rule is to make sure (by a photographic record or script notes) that the characters, subject or object are in the same position at the end of one shot as at the beginning of the next shot.

When a new scene is introduced with no action taking place at the beginning, you are free to commence that shot anywhere.

ANALOGY—SCENE PERSPECTIVE

In composing a scene, consider the way we use our sense of sight in real life.

We see things from one place, or move nearer to something and do not concentrate on seeing more, but less, of a broad view.

We may not focus attention on any one particular thing with a wide field of vision before us. The whole scene as we concentrate upon it is visible.

It is only when we concentrate on one portion that the detail becomes the center of interest.

Our eyes, being very flexible, work closely with our brain and concentrate upon the whole or any part thereof.

We can change focus or move across the scene as fast or as slowly as we wish.

The angle from which we view the scene—closeness or distance of viewpoint, and the sequence in which successive pictures are presented —is determined, broadly speaking, by a consideration of the way in which an on-looker would use his eyes were he viewing the scene in real life.

We must use imagination to determine what the camera will "see" for the viewer to interpret the "message" credibly to the viewer.

EXAMPLES—FUNDAMENTAL "RULES" OF COMPOSITION

WRONG   **RIGHT**

(31) Too much space between subjects.

(32) By bringing subjects closer together, the relationship of the characters is better emphasized.

(33) Frame-line cuts the actor's head, thus detracting from the intended shot.

(34) The proper framing places emphasis on the actor and thus does not detract from the story.

(35) Too much background material draws attention to itself and away from the actor and action.

(36) A de-emphasized background aids story development and creates focus.

EXAMPLES—FUNDAMENTAL "RULES" OF COMPOSITION

WRONG   **RIGHT**

(37) The space to the right of the girl draws the emphasis from the characters and to itself. The space is not significant in this shot.

(38) Coupled with the body positions of the actors and their line of sight, the space to the right of the girl now is significant. It creates anticipation in the audience.

(39) Here the camera is too "tight" resulting in "cut-off." Again the framing draws attention to itself.

(40) By correct camera placement the framing emphasizes the story only.

(41) This camera placement results in "loose" framing and an uninteresting angle. It lacks emphasis.

(42) From a different angle, framing and emphasis are now "sharpened." The interest is achieved.

Chapter 16

READY? "ROLL! ACTION!"

BUT BEFORE YOU ROLL THE CAMERA . . .

Scripting, photography and editing are bound together. Editing begins as soon as you start to break down a scene into its component shots.

When final editing takes place, make sure that the change of viewpoint is neither too abrupt nor too gradual. A sudden change from a distant shot to an extreme close-up may bewilder the audience and make it difficult for them to relate the scene to what follows.

PROCEDURE IN EDITING

The exposed footage is developed and processed in a laboratory. The negative is left intact. The positive (print or copy from the negative) is the processed footage to be edited.

The negative and positive are then coded to match the frames. When this is accomplished you will be ready to assemble the footage.

Editing film is the joining together of the picture and sound and effects in synchronization ("sync"), from the footages slated and tapes recorded, and then made ready for editing as dictated by the script. Editing film is a selective process.

"Bits" and "pieces" of film contain a number which identifies the order of the scenes. The same scene may be broken up into a number of "takes."

The same or different scenes are taken from different angles and distances, particularly where the story involves people and a plot. Editing film footage may be analyzed the same as cutting diamonds. The wrong cut can ruin the diamond. The wrong cut can also ruin a scene and story.

YOU, JOHN DOE, AS A FILM-MAKER

There are many important decisions to make before you "roll" the camera.

Decide what kind of scenes you will need to execute your ideas. Consider the length of each scene. Some need to be short, some long. Decide on a location for each scene.

Consider arranging the order of the scenes in continuity in a sequence, then consider the arrangement of the transitions between sequences.

It is your responsibility to make the best selection of the scene to scene footage. In editing, you can direct the audience's attention to what you want it to see at any given moment.

The movement of the scenes, the staging, can be designed to create the maximum experience in terms of the substance of the manuscript. By the use of lighting, color, imaginative design, choice of props and locations, a specific personal experience can be created for an audience.

Creative energy can only be put to the fullest use and the imagination stimulated when one cares deeply about the content of the subject and manuscript.

It has meaning when the originator-interpreter is courageous and hopefully inspired to project the action. Technique is a necessity, inspiration, a blessing.

When you are ready to start filming, make sure you know all the basics of use of your equipment. What equipment will you need? How much of it? Sound, camera, motion picture or still camera, audio recorder, videotape recorder. What kind of lenses and special camera attachments, tripods, filters, diffusion devices, photographic accessories? What film stock do you need? How much exterior? How much interior?

What about developing and processing? The film laboratory plays an essential role in the transition from conception of story, plot or theme to the finished product—the film.

What about lighting? What kind of lighting equipment, cables and connectors, stands and accessories?

Consider the mechanics of film making. There are music, special effects, titles, sound effects that enhance your film idea. Be careful not to distract. Remember that the film is for an audience.

Atmosphere footage must be rolled by the sound engineer and identified for the place—interior or exterior. The footage needed must be turned over to the film editor.

Strive for technical excellence. The story often depends upon the creative application of technical excellence.

BASIC UNDERSTANDING OF THE CINEMATIC TECHNIQUE

You should present the material so that the footage flows in a sequential and natural order. Eliminate redundant action. Remove insignificant footage and condense your material to the essential and significant. You may consider changing the order of the scenes if you feel the result will be more effective to help develop the story.

You must know when to linger on a scene and when to move quickly, remembering that it is often unnecessary to show the whole of the action.

Be careful of bad matching, particularly in close-up shots of people.

You must put yourself into the position of the audience. Ask yourself, "Is the story told in a clear and interesting manner and is the environment and background properly established? Where would I want to look next, if I were watching this scene in real life?

BASIC UNDERSTANDING OF LIGHTING

Lighting has two main purposes:

1. To illuminate for a satisfactory picture;

2. To achieve artistic effect.

At times the technical and artistic factors conflict and it is necessary to compromise.

Compensate for sharp contrasts. The picture detail results from illumination, composition and contrast. Contrast however, must be controlled. For example, a man wearing a dark suit standing before a black background is "lost."

The form of composition is determined by depth of field and the size of the images occupying the frame. The perspective of the composition concerns the appearance of objects in respect to their relative distance, meaning and position. These are only some of the factors in which light assumes control of the picture.

Natural source lighting includes, daylight, sunlight, firelight, moonlight, gaslight, candlelight, lamplight and reflective light from an indirect source.

Effective lighting includes silhouette, low-key, dusk, dawn, night and shadows. For film, a playing area is set up for specific action in each shot. That area is marked, rigged and focused by control devices of each unit of light as it is set to project intensity or as it is diffused for less intensity.

Lighting itself is a source of mood. It helps to create an atmosphere. It supports the environment. Lighting for effect and to affect a natural projection is creative work.

CASTING

Assuming that a suitable, well-organized script is available, the first step is casting the show. After this has been carried out, the rehearsals should be organized by a production assistant.

SCRIPT

The script should be marked with stage business, the basic camera angles and actor positions. The director should analyze the character and intent of the script well in advance so that he may make the emotional elements of the drama clear to his cast and team members.

SET DESIGN—PLAYING AREA—LOCATION OR SETTING

The director should prepare a rough sketch of the set. The backgrounds (interiors and exteriors) natural settings or areas specially set up for photography should be discussed in relation to the color and contrast of the wearing apparel of the cast, source lighting and changes that may occur in the source light such as the movement of the sun.

The properties, construction, rentals, loans, purchases, special props and other such details must be taken from the script in advance.

SOUND EFFECTS—PICTURE EFFECTS—TITLES

Sound effects and picture effects should be marked in the script where they occur and ordered through the editor. Main titles and credits are ordered through the editor or set up with an optical studio.

MUSIC

Background music should be marked in the script where it begins, ends and segues.

The music librarian, music editor or editor should choose the exact selections needed (from a music film library). The editor works closely in association with the director. The use of music not in the public domain requires permission from the copyright proprietor.

ACTORS IN REHEARSAL

The basic rule for the director in dramatic rehearsals is to devote the most time and energy on those portions of the story which best express the heart of the production.

The director, after careful analysis of intention, translates the same into visual terms. He prepares the action and the motivations for each actor in the cast. All positions the actor will take are pre-set and marked for focus, sound perspective and light.

The director should be able to interpret the basic requirements and limitations the actor must remember. The camera will record only what it is aimed at and focused upon. Sound will only be effective if its perspective will be accomplished.

PLAYING FOR THE CAMERA LENSES
AND FRAME-LINE TECHNIQUE

From every perspective, the actor has one main consideration, to truthfully portray the character role.

If the actor is fully versed in all aspects of his character, then he has little to worry about. However, if he is not well versed, then it does little good to say that he must play for the camera, for playing for the camera comes out of his characterization.

His timing must coincide with the camera movement, and his motivation and concentration provide him with the necessary elements needed for the close-up where every single detail is photographically recorded to be seen and felt. By the very nature of the frame-line technique, he must remain in character at all times.

All positions the actor will take are pre-set so that he is in sharp focus at all times with every movement. His image will fade, become over or under-exposed, blur out of focus and be distorted if the marked positions that are pre-set for photography are not adhered to. The actor must play for the areas pre-lighted for the positions he will take in every scene. If an actor suddenly takes it upon himself to change a position during the take, he may not only move himself out of perspective but also destroy the realism of the entire scene.

For the stage, there are nine designated playing areas. The lighting changes, during the progress of the play, in accordance with the requirements of the drama.

The lighting and intensity will be prepared to compensate for the camera operation as pre-set by the lighting technician and the cameraman.

In motion picture production, as in live television, a playing area is set up for a specific action. The lens is calibrated to follow the movement and focus.

PLAYING FOR THE MICROPHONE

The microphone is a sensitive instrument but it has some limitations, even if it's the finest electronic equipment available. While the actor is not required to have a technical knowledge of this instrument's capabilities in transmitting his voice, he should have an understanding of what he must do when dialogue and speech are involved. Subtle asides must be carefully expressed, because, if they are spoken too softly, the microphone cannot possibly pick them up.

Movement in and throughout the setting must be made with care, for the microphone can pick up sounds of movement which the ear normally does not hear. "Control" is the key word for the actor playing for the microphone, for control results in a finished product. Without control of voice and movement, the entire production loses its dramatic emphasis and becomes superficial. Sound perspective and voice level must be maintained at all times.

The actor must be guided to discipline his interpretation throughout the entire drama for frame-line and film technique.

CAMERA BLOCKING

In the cinematic media, the actor is met with the camera or the camera moves to meet him. He is defined in the lights and shadows of the environment and his voice is electronically "mixed" with the sounds of the atmosphere around him.

The setting, lights, camera and equipment are extremely important if all the instruments of the arts are to be counted upon to effectively communicate the drama to the audience.

The camera is the liaison between the actor and the screen. Therefore, the director should establish the whole scene before the camera, thus allowing the camera complete freedom of movement within the setting.

Camera, sound and scene blocking are usually devoted to the physical placement of the camera, setting of the lenses and camera logistics within the set. The blocking period is designed for the lighting technicians as well as for the actors. All concerned become acquainted with the needs of the director and allow for the limitations of the settings and studio space.

Scene blocking involves positioning actors, camera, lights and mikes within a setting in order to capture on film the director's interpretation of the story. To plan the blocking, the story is broken down into units of action or scenes. The blocking is then done, scene by scene, with due regard to overall continuity of sound and picture.

The camera is pointed at what the audience should see. The eye levels are dictated by the physical needs and design of what the character sees, for the camera is his eyes.

The angle of vision is not determined solely by the spectator's position in the auditorium, but by the infinite variety of angles from which the camera observes the scene. The point of view must always be selected for a specific purpose and meaning.

There is a direct relationship between the audience, the object, the images and the theme. Some directors stage their actors in such a manner that they are "captured" by the camera. Others move their cameras so that the characters are always in the frame. The interpretation of the movement, camera to actor or actor to camera, is a matter of the director's style.

PROCEDURE—"ROLL ACTION!" JOHN DOE

"Slate" your takes and scenes and sound *before* each take—not *after* the scene is "rolled" for action.

When you roll for action:

1. "ROLL" camera and sound, camera first. Camera is rolling.

2. Watch for the cameraman and soundman to signal when camera speed is in sync with the recorder.

3. Slate the scene first, clap stick to record and mark film and tape.

4. Signal "ACTION" to the actors.

The scene is in progress. It is "quiet" except for the action of the drama. At the end of the take, after the camera is "CUT"—

5. Remember to freeze your actors in their last action and position until the cameraman checks their positions through the viewfinder, verifying that they are in the focus pre-set for them.

6. The soundman, too, will report the recording of the sound as acceptable or not.

7. When this is accomplished and the scene is acceptable to the director, the script supervisor should record on a scene form (the scene report) descriptive notes as necessary for the editor and director.

8. The assistant cameraman will also record on a form (the camera report) the footage and his information for camera reports to the laboratory.

DO'S TO REMEMBER . . .

- Remember to mark your script for the "action." Line the script accordingly, taking credit for the scenes and action filmed.

- Use a variety of shots, "cut-ins" and "cut-aways" for variety and interest and for developing the actions as necessary.

- Most important to remember is the "MASTER" shot. All of the scene is taken in one angle as a basic reference—WHAT, WHERE, and WHY.

- Remember to use the "close-up" shot to render a meaning for your subject.

- Remember that smooth-flowing continuity in the action and story structure depend upon matching exactly the preceding shots with the succeeding shots. Note every action accordingly.

- "Lap-over" new scenes with the "dove-tailing" scene.

- Plan every scene structure and sequence structure along with where the transitions will be effected.

- Remember to consider the length of the scenes to be arranged into the sequence and transition.

- Remember the fundamentals of the basic equipment you will be using. Understand the use, capabilities and limitations of the various lenses.

- Remember to roll the recorder for some atmosphere footage—25, 50, 100 or other feet. The editor needs this footage. He can advise how much.

- Remember the fundamental rules of composition.

"DON'TS" TO REMEMBER . . .

- Don't cut from one angle or distance to another only very slightly different from it.

- On the other hand, don't cut from extreme long shot to big close-up; it will be jarring.

- Don't cut a portion out of the middle of a piece of action and continue straight on—always disguise the break by inserting another shot.

- Don't join two shots so that the same piece of action is seen twice.

- Don't fade-out and then cut to a normal, fully exposed shot—follow with a fade-in.

- Don't allow any shot to remain so long on the screen that the audience is conscious of waiting for the next one.

- Don't show a character, who is supposed to be moving in one direction, crossing the screen first one way and, immediately afterwards, the other.

- Don't follow a left pan with a right pan. You will confuse the audience and yourself.

- Don't show long, unessential pieces of action in full.

- Don't leave a shot in unless it fulfills a meaning of the story.

- Don't allow an audience to become aware of the camera at any time.

A FEW LAST WORDS . . .

We are only in the early stages of the era of audio-visual communication. In the rapidly developing technology of our society, the audio-visual media are as much a part of our everyday living as the telephone and the pen and pencil. Already there is the prediction of the computerization of shopping and banking and inventory, and of television-telephones. Video recording for the home is now as much an accomplished fact as the audio tape recorder. Consequently, the business of communicating through the audio-visual media is the concern of every John Doe and will continue to grow in importance and use.

The media are no longer centered only in the large cities. As equipment for production and consumption becomes more easily available, production and consumption become more and more decentralized. They become important to all who wish to instruct, train, entertain or communicate with others.

From Hollywood to John Doe may seem to have been a long step, but the step has already been taken, and you, John Doe, who seek to develop your role as a writer, director, originator-interpreter, and whose intention is to acquire experience must be prepared to use the media effectively and creatively.

❀   ❀   ❀

APPENDIX

BASIC FORMS
FOR PRODUCTION PLANNING

Included in the appendix are several forms which are useful in planning and production. Though the forms may differ somewhat with each production agency, the organization and items presented here are typical.

STORYBOARD

BASIC FORM OF THE STORYBOARD—Is a device which tells the story through illustrations drawn in perspective. Through the storyboard, the director, producer **and** production personnel can visualize shots and scenes in continuity as a development of the story.

#

_____
_____
_____
_____
_____
_____

#

_____
_____
_____
_____
_____

#

_____
_____
_____
_____
_____
_____

#

_____
_____
_____
_____
_____
_____

SHOOTING SCHEDULE

BASIC FORM OF A SHOOTING SCHEDULE—Is a day and date schedule which is pre-planned by an assistant director or unit manager to include scenes and settings, props, cast, wardrobe and production requirements.

Project:_____   Est. Shooting Days_____

SHOOTING SCHEDULE

TITLE:_____   PRODUCER_____

_____   DIRECTOR_____

DAYS IN SCHEDULE_____ PLUS_____ TOTAL_____ CAMERAMAN_____

SETTING (int) (ext)_____   SOUND   _____

DAY & DATE	SCENES	SILENT—SOUND	CAST	PROPS	WARDROBE

DAILY PRODUCTION SCHEDULE

BASIC FORM OF THE PRODUCTION SCHEDULE
and daily shooting schedules are planned by the assistant director and unit manager cooperatively. The script
supervisor may also do this.

DAILY PRODUCTION SCHEDULE

WORKING TITLE: _____

No. DAYS
ESTIMATED: _____ No. OF DAYS ON PICTURE INCLUDING TODAY: _____

LOCATION: _____ IDLE: _____
  Fair
  Cloudy   WORK: _____ TOTAL DAYS: _____
  Rain

SETTING: _____ DATE: _____
  (int.)
  (ext.)   DATE STARTED: _____
                  ESTIMATED FINISH DATE: _____

DIRECTOR: _____

PRODUCER: _____

TIME STARTED: _____ LUNCH FROM: _____ TILL: _____ TIME FINISHED: __
SOUND CALL: _____ M.O.S. _____ OTHER: _____
SCENES IN SCRIPT: _____ MINUTES ON FILM TO DATE: _____
TAKEN PREVIOUS: _____ RETAKES: _____
TAKEN TODAY: _____ ADDED SCENES: _____
TOTAL TO DATE: _____ STILLS: _____
SCENES TO BE TAKEN: _____
_____

SCENE NO.																			
RETAKES:																			
ADDED SCENES:																			

      PICTURE NEGATIVE   SOUND NEGATIVE

USED PREVIOUS: _____ _____
USED TODAY: _____ _____
USED TO DATE: _____ _____
DRAWN: _____ _____
ON HAND: _____ _____

              ADVANCE SCHEDULE

DATE: _____   SETTING: _____
                              (ext.)
REMARKS: _____   (int.)
                         LOCATION: _____
                              (ext.)
(signed) _____ (int.)

SCENE REPORT

BASIC FORM OF A SCENE REPORT — Notes as
stated must be made on production information during
shooting. This is the duty of the script supervisor. The
information recorded is then used by director and film
editor.

SCENE REPORT

TITLE: _____   DAY & DATE: _____

SETTING: _____

SCENE	TAKE	D E S C R I P T I O N (circle good takes)	Production Note

BUDGET FORM

BASIC FORM OF THE BUDGET—The production budget is planned by the unit manager and the producer in consultation with other production personnel.

		35mm _____ 16mm _____ 8mm _____	Color _____ B&W _____

TITLE: _____ PROJECT: _____

BUDGET FORM

CLASSIFICATION	Estimated	Actual	pg. ref.
(A) STORY			
1. Research Services			
2. Consultants - Advisors			
3. Writers			
4. Storyboard-Materials-Typing			
5. Other			
(B) PRODUCTION			
1. Production Personnel			
2. Photography materials & Film			
3. Sound materials & Tape			
4. Property materials & purchase			
5. Construction & materials			
6. Studio & Sets & Dressing			
7. Location & Setting & Dressing			
8. Crew Personnel			
9. Equipment Rentals & Purchase			
10. Accessories-Camera-Lights			
11. Miscellaneous			
12. Other			
(C) CASTING			
1. Narration & Voices			
2. Principals			
3. Bits & Parts			
4. Background & Extras			
5. Animals & Children			
6. Other			
(D) LABORATORY			
1. Developing & processing			
2. Work print & Cinex			
3. Coding & Edge numbering			
4. Sound transfers			
5. Fine grains - Interpositives			
6. Reduction (16mm) (8mm)			
7. Color or B & W			
8. Answer print			
9. Other services			
(E) MUSIC AND SOUND EFFECTS			
1. Live			
2. Library music			
3. Music & Sound effects			
4. Other			

BUDGET FORM (cont'd)

CLASSIFICATION	ESTIMATED	ACTUAL	pg. ref.
(F) SOUND TRACK — RECORDING & MIX			
1. Recording Studio & Personal			
2. Stock & Tape materials			
3. Transfers			
4. Dubbing			
5. Other Services			
(G) EDITING SERVICES			
1. Work print - Picture & Track			
2. Coding preparation			
3. Syncing dialogue			
4. Narration & Voices			
5. First Cut - Subsequent cuts			
6. Final Cut			
7. Music & Sound Effects			
8. Picture Effects			
9. Library & Stock Footage			
10. Preparing track-picture (A&B)			
11. Pull negative			
12. Record-Mix-Transfers			
13. Matching Negative			
14. Cutting Room & Facilities			
15. Supplies, leader, purchases			
16. Equipment & Rentals			
17. Editor & Personnel			
18. Other Services			
(H) OPTICALS—TITLES—ART WORK			
1. Graphics			
2. Photography & Effects			
3. Art Work			
4. Titles			
5. Animation			
6. Materials & Supplies & Services			
7. Optical Effects			
8. Other Services			
(I) PRODUCTION ADMINISTRATION			
1. Insurance			
2. Transportation & Freight			
3. Shipping & Handling			
4. Travel & Perdiem			
5. Office, telephone, services			
6. Paycheck & bookeeping services			
7. Administration contingencies			
8. Production contingencies			
9. Other			

BIBLIOGRAPHY

There are few books devoted solely to film production techniques. You may find help in books on theater and stage techniques, in areas such as scenic design, lighting, stagecraft, make-up, etc., but all such information must be adapted for film.

A brief reference list is appended to this book to give you a start in your study of film technique. It includes only those books devoted solely to film production and names of some equipment manufacturers, film laboratories and sales organizations which provide helpful, up-to-date information concerning equipment, processes and new technological developments. This list is neither definitive nor exhaustive, but is rather a suggestion for the beginning of a study which will last as long as your interest in the audio-visual media lasts.

BOOKS

ALTON, JOHN. *Painting with Light* (Macmillan and Company: New York), 1949. Studio camera techniques with particular emphasis on lighting. Includes interior and exterior shooting.

BRANSTON, BRIAN. *Film Maker's Guide to Planning, Directing and Shooting Films for Pleasure and Profit* (Hillary House Publishers: New York), 1968

BRETZ, RUDY. *Techniques of Television Production* (McGraw-Hill: New York), 1962

BRODBECK, EMIL E. *Handbook of Basic Motion Picture Techniques* (Chilton Book Company: Philadelphia), 1966
Movie and Videotape Special Effects (Chilton Book Company: Philadelphia), 1968

BURDER, JOHN. *Technique of Editing 16mm Films* (Hastings House Publishers: New York), 1968

EISLER, HANS. *Composing for the Films* (Oxford University Press: New York), 1947. A theoretical base for film music.

FRAYNE, JOHN G. and HALLEY, WOLFE. *Elements of Sound Recording* (Wiley and Sons: New York), 1949. Recording techniques, including both magnetic and stereophonic sound.

GORDON, JAY E. *Motion-Picture Production for Industry* (Macmillan and Company: New York), 1961

HOPPE, I. BERNARD. *Basic Motion Picture Technology* (Hastings House Publishers: New York), 1970

KRACAUER, SIEGFRIED. *Theory of Film* (Oxford University Press: New York), 1960

LAWSON, JOHN HOWARD. *Film: the Creative Process; the Search for an Audio-Visual Language and Structure* (Hill and Wang: New York), 1964

LONDON, KURT. *Film Music.* (Arno Press Inc.: New York), reprint of 1936 edition

MANCHELL, FRANK. *Movies and How They Are Made* (Prentice-Hall: Englewood Cliffs, N. J.), 1968. For grades three-seven.

MASCELLI, JOSEPH U. *Five C's of Cinematography* (Cinegraphic: Hollywood, California), 1965

NAPIER, FRANK. *Noises Off London* (Fredrick Muller: London), 1936. A handbook of sound effects.

NILSEN, VLADIMER. *The Cinema as a Graphic Art* (Hill and Wang: New York), 1959. The creative uses of the camera and the dynamics of composition.

REISZ, KAREL. *The Technique of Film Editing* (Focal Press: New York, London), 1964, 1958. Editing in relation to directing, script and sound.

STARR, CECILE, ed. *Ideas on Film: A Handbook for the 16mm Film User* (Funk and Wagnalls: New York), 1951

Technique of the Motion Picture Camera: Library of Communication (Hastings House Publishers: New York), 1967

WALTER, ERNST. *Technique of the Film Cutting Room* (Hastings House Publishers: New York), 1969

WHEELER, LESLIE J. *Principles of Cinematography* (Morgan and Morgan, Inc.: Hastings-on-Hudson, N. Y.), 1969

RESOURCES

Association of Cinema Laboratories
1925 K Street, N.W., Washington, D.C.
Handbook of *Recommended Standards
and Procedures for Motion Picture
Laboratories* is available.

Bell and Howell Company
Chicago, Illinois

Byron Motion Pictures, Inc.
1226 Wisconsin Ave., N.W.
Washington, D.C.

Camera Equipment Company, Inc.
315 West 43rd Street
New York, N.Y.

Camera Service Center
333 W. 52nd Street
New York, N.Y.

Century Lighting, Inc.
521 W. 43rd Street
New York, N.Y.

Consolidated Film Industries
959 Seward Street
Hollywood, California

Eastman Kodak Company
Rochester, New York
How To Make Good Movies
(series of booklets)

Florman & Babb, Inc.
New York, N.Y.

Jack A. Frost
234 Piquette Street
Detroit, Michigan

Kliegl Bros.
321 W 50th Street
New York, N.Y.

Mark Armistead, Inc.
Camera and Motion Picture Equipment
1041 North Formosa
Hollywood, California

Midwest Stage Lighting
55 West Wacker Drive
Chicago, Illinois

INDEX

281